I/Eu

Universitas Press
Montreal

www.universitaspress.com

Modern Classics Editor: Cristina Artenie

First published in August 2025

Work published with the support of the National Library Foundation of the Ministry of Culture of Brazil and the Guimarães Rosa Institute of the Ministry of Foreign Affairs of Brazil.
Obra publicada com o apoio da Fundação Biblioteca Nacional, do Ministério da Cultura do Brasil, e do Instituto Guimarães Rosa, do Ministério das Relações Exteriores do Brasil.

Library and Archives Canada Cataloguing in Publication

Title: I-EU : and other poems / Augusto dos Anjos ; edited and translated by Maurício Búrigo.
Names: Anjos, Augusto dos, 1884-1914, author | Búrigo, Maurício, editor, translator. | Container of (work): Anjos, Augusto dos, 1884-1914. Eu. Selections. | Container of (expression): Anjos, Augusto dos, 1884-1914. Eu. Selections. English.
Description: Contains selected poems from Eu and other poems published posthumously. | Poems in Portuguese with English translation.
Identifiers: Canadiana 20250242680 | ISBN 9781988963723 (softcover)
Subjects: LCSH: Anjos, Augusto dos, 1884-1914—Translations into English. | LCGFT: Poetry.
Classification: LCC PQ9697.A75 A2 2025 | DDC 869.1/41—dc23

Augusto dos Anjos

I/Eu
and other poems

Selected and translated by Maurício Búrigo

Universitas Press
Montreal

Augusto dos Anjos, 1912

TABLE OF CONTENTS

vii
Alcebiades Diniz Miguel — Like an Anatomy Lesson: The Fierce, Mystical Entropy of Augusto dos Anjos
xix
Chronology
xxv
Maurício Búrigo — Translator's Note

1
I/Eu

2	3
Monólogo de uma Sombra	Monologue of a Shadow
18	19
O Morcego	The Bat
20	21
Psicologia de um Vencido	Psychology of a Loser
22	23
A Idéia	The Idea
24	25
Idealização da Humanidade Futura	Idealization of Future Humanity
26	27
As Cismas do Destino	The Misgivings of Destiny
64	65
Solitário	Solitary
66	67
Idealismo	Idealism
68	69
Último Credo	Last Creed
70	71
Solilóquio de um Visionário	Soliloquy of a Visionary
72	73
Vozes da Morte	Voices of Death
74	75
O Martírio do Artista	Martyrdom of the Artist
76	77
Vozes de um Túmulo	Voices from a Tomb
78	79
Vandalismo	Vandalism

80	81
Versos Íntimos	Intimate Verses
82	83
Eterna Mágoa	Eternal Woe
84	85
O Lamento das Coisas	The Lament of Things
86	87
Apóstrofe à Carne	Apostrophe to the Flesh
88	89
Suprême Convulsion	Suprême Convulsion
90	91
À um Gérmen	To a Germ
92	93
A Floresta	The Forest
94	95
O Poeta do Hediondo	The Poet of the Hideous
96	97
Numa Forja	At a Forge
104	105
Vítima do Dualismo	Victim of Dualism
106	127
Ao Luar	In the Moonlight
108	109
Anseio	Anxiety
110	111
O Último Número	The Last Number

113
Critical assessments on Augusto dos Anjos

Like an Anatomy Lesson:
The Fierce, Mystical Entropy of Augusto dos Anjos

> *Up looked the body: flesh, order, and preservation summoned. He smiled and hardened again; withdrawing already, he looked at the house: what had happened? What had been mankind's way thus far? An effort to bring order into something that should have remained play. But after all, it had remained play in the end, for nothing had reality. Did he have reality? No; all he had was every possibility. He bedded his neck deeper into the may-weed that smelled of thyrse and Walpurgis. Melting through the noon-day, his head pebbled, brooklike.* (Benn 9)

Introduction: The Contemplation of Horror

A singularly intense—one might even say brutal—moment in *The Republic*, Plato's great treatise on justice, occurs when he introduces his readers to horror, in Book IV, while discussing the distinction between the two hemispheres of the soul—according to Socrates—the rational (the aspect that reasons, thus representing rational control) and the irrational, "with which it loves, hungers, thirsts, and feels the flutter and titillation of other desires" (Plato 397-399). In illustrating this opposition, which is quite common in Platonic thought, Socrates, the central character, shares a unique story that is worth reproducing in its entirety:

> "But," I said, "I once heard a story which I believe, that Leontius the son of Aglaïon, on his way up from the Peiraeus under the outer side of the northern wall, becoming aware of dead bodies that lay at the place of public execution at the same time felt a desire to see them and a repugnance and aversion, and that for a time he resisted and veiled his head, but overpowered in despite of all by his desire, with wide staring eyes he rushed up to the corpses and cried, 'There, ye wretches, take your fill of the fine spectacle!'" (Plato 399-401)

Although Plato addresses abstract concepts related to rationality and irrationality within the human soul, he does not hesitate to employ this "anecdote" (as he refers to it), a

Like an Anatomy Lesson

brief narrative imbued with terror, to illustrate the central point of his argument—the journey of a living terror, a shiver felt by the body, which transitions into the abstract realms of philosophical discourse. To this uniquely tortuous path, Plato adds an additional element: the horror in this passage is not derived from a decaying or decomposing body—a natural process that might only disturb the exceptionally sensitive—but from a *twisted* body, one destroyed by torture and left for carrion animals outside the city. In fact, it is the appearance of these bodies after the inflicted torture that most captivates Leontius's attention; it is what he truly *desires* to contemplate. This narrative shift by Plato is brief, as it conveys a sense of Leontius's anxiety to the reader, who also yearns to gaze upon such bodies. However, this desire is thwarted as the anecdote concludes abruptly, leaving only Leontius's decision, while Plato continues with his exposition.

In any case, Plato's exploration of horror seems to illustrate a philosophical inclination to contemplate terror. He could demonstrate the conflict between opposing natures—one rational and the other irrational—through any desire capable of engaging the human senses and displacing the will. However, the Greek philosopher emphasized this anecdote to highlight not only the allure of violence but also the necessity of horror (even in the form of exemplification) for the development of philosophical abstractions. It is as if horror provides a jolt of reality that makes certain ideas tangible and perceptible to our consciousness and senses.

However, if this brief excerpt from *The Republic* reveals the profound connections between terror—particularly corporal terror—and speculative thought, what remains unclear is the outcome of the anecdote recounted by Socrates: what truly happened to Leontius? A cunning narrator, Plato interrupts the account of Aglaion's son's vision of the bodies at the very moment the outcome is imminent, precisely at the climax. But what would this encounter be like, after all? What would be the perception—perhaps poetic—of these corpses, torn apart by torture, through Leontius's eyes? What would it be like to have a maddened Plato, who would pierce his philosophical arguments with terrifying images of bodies and decay? A similar phenomenon was not produced in Ancient Greece, but rather in Brazil, by the poet Augusto dos Anjos (1884-1914), who poetically transformed the speculative discourse of philosophy through the tremors provoked by horror and disgust.

I. Modern Buddhism

Augusto de Carvalho Rodrigues dos Anjos, the poet's given name, was born on April 20, 1884, in a small town within the municipality of Sapé, Paraíba, known as Engenho Pau d'Arco. He began his education at home under the guidance of his father and later attended the Lyceu Parahybano, where he would eventually become a professor in 1908. After completing his studies, he pursued a law degree at the Recife Law School from 1903 to 1907, earning his bachelor's degree. In 1910, he married Ester Fialho, and the couple had three children, one of whom tragically passed away at seven months. The poet died far from his native Paraíba, in the city of Leopoldina, Minas Gerais, on November 12, 1914, at the age of 30. The official cause of death was pneumonia, which was not surprising, as he had been struggling with tuberculosis for several years.

> Whence does it come? From whatever
> Crude matter comes this light falling sur
> Nebulae of unknown crypts, mysterious,
> Like the stalactites inside a cavern?
>
> Comes from the psychogenetic and stern
> Battle of a fascicle of molecules nervous
> Which, in disintegrations marvelous,
> Deliberates, and then wants and exerts!

On the one hand, this original vision deepens Schopenhauerian pessimism while countering the eventual optimistic positivism of Spencer and Haeckel, as well as the Darwinian determinism that arises from the strict application of the principles on the survival of the fittest as a metaphysical axiom. On the other, the poet introduces Spengler and his apocalyptic theorization into the discussion as well. Conversely, Augusto dos Anjos subjected his thoughts to Aristotelian methodological rigor, employing a precise systematization that rendered his poetic language both strange and exact. The words of Augusto dos Anjos were not mere decorative embellishments or refined choices of verbal craftsmanship, akin to those found in Parnassian poetry, which was popular in Brazil at the beginning of the 20th century. Instead, the words in poems like the example above express concepts that are as dark as they are knowable—moreover, they are dizzyingly strange and singular, shocking even to the readers and critics of the author's time. In this sense, within this peculiar staging of a tragedy of universal thought (at least within a specific historical context) presented in verse form, there is a final *plot twist*: in a last and desperate philosophical turn, his intense pessimistic materialism transforms into a kind of mysticism of entropy and disintegration. In a certain way, Augusto dos Anjos' thought, despite its materialist essence, seems to encompass a perception of *truth*—or at least a potential truth—that aligns closely with the notion of sacrifice.

The only book of poetry by Augusto dos Anjos published during his lifetime is titled *Eu* ["I"]. The cover features a diffuse pinkish background, with the enormous letters of the title prominently displayed in bold red, evoking the geometric roughness characteristic of *Art Deco*. This work is not merely a monument to solipsism; rather, it offers a subjective perspective on the objective philosophical vision presented by the poet: the inexorable, universal decay, conveyed through a unique musicality and a vocabulary that is both exotic and, at times, shocking and almost repulsive. This book can be regarded as the poet's ultimate sacrifice: he invested all his meager savings and agreed to leave his native Paraíba to embark on an adventure as a freelance private tutor in Rio de Janeiro, solely to oversee the printing of his work. This printing was made possible thanks to the financial support of his brother, Odilon dos Anjos.[*] However, exile in the former capital of Brazil proved to be devastating for Augusto dos Anjos; it not only deteriorated his health but also intensified the unique nihilism that his poetry conveys—a profound disappointment with the provincialism of Paraíba and an unrelenting revolt against the social injustices plaguing Brazil. This sentiment is corroborated by friends who lived with the poet during that time, such as Francisco de Assis and José Oiticica. Augusto dos Anjos clung to his sole book as the very embodiment of his ideas, although later, more comprehensive editions reveal that he was already organizing additional works, both poetic and prose. The developments of his work in the landscape of Brazilian poetry during the 1910s were marked by numerous 'pre' and 'post' distinctions in relation to Modernism and its aspirations to redefine Brazilian culture. The distinctiveness of Augusto dos Anjos' poetry, in contrast to the supposed modernist 'renewal' and the 'goldsmithing of the word' advocated by the previous generation of Parnassians and Symbolists, is remarkable and will be thoroughly examined in the following segment.

II. Poetics of the slaughterhouse and/or the cemetery

It is now time to confront the book *Eu* and the poems it contains, which seem to defy not only the conventional rules of theme and taste (even within modernist canons) but also remain a unique and extremely popular work. Following the ill-fated yet now-cherished *editio princeps*, it has undergone numerous re-editions and stands alongside much better-known and beloved poets of Brazilian literature, such as Carlos Drummond de Andrade, Castro Alves, and Manuel Bandeira. In this context, the growing popularity of Augusto dos Anjos since his death presents a mystery. The entirety of the poems in *Eu* (as well as other poems collected in later and posthumous editions) exhibits a series

---

[*] After the author's death, 46 poems collected by his friend Órris Soares were added to the original set of the book's first edition. This edition became the foundation for the author's expanded work, titled *Eu e outras poesias* ["I and other poems"].

of characteristics that are rarely found among authors of popular works. First, there is a *distinctive language*; second, the *verbal iconography* is unique to these poems; and finally, the *general meaning* evoked by the poet—what this poetry, rich in strangeness, seeks to elicit in the reader's experience—create a profound engagement with these merciless verses, inviting an effort to understand them.

Thus, the *language* of Augusto dos Anjos is the initial impact of his poetry. At first glance, he is a poet who vigorously adhered to the formalism of his time—represented by the descriptive poetry of Parnassianism and the symbolic and suggestive evocation of Symbolism. Likewise, this author used the sonnet as his favorite format for his poetic constructions with the frequent use, as highlighted by the critic and researcher João Adolfo Hansen, of techniques related to the decasyllabic—his verses are long, with a complex and varied sonority (see Hansen 20-21), with the frequent use of *enjambments* (a method of vocalic extension of the verse, widely used in Parnassian poetry in Brazil) and strange caesuras in the cutting of the verses. Added to this is the high level of erudition in the vocabulary adopted by Augusto dos Anjos in his poems: these are expressions derived from history, mythology, and literature (as well as other arts), but also from physics, chemistry, biology, philosophy, and theology. This is a broad arsenal of erudite expressions and words that are functional in their specific fields and that the poet uses quite frequently but in a completely natural way within the fluidity of the verses and the construction of the images evoked in the figures of speech of his poems. That is not, therefore, the empty Parnassian erudition or the sometimes abstruse and impenetrable Symbolist construction; Augusto dos Anjos, in this sense, is the architect of a materialist, scientific language, but quite clear in a certain sense—even in its darkest moments, the shock of the rawness of the images serves as a bridge for the reader to understand the layers of thought evoked in such a poetic construction. In this sense—and this will be something we will see later—Augusto dos Anjos found companions in other literary traditions outside of Brazil, in this strange language, extremely musical but evocative of what seem to be fierce terrors, existential and philosophical dead ends in individual and collective terms.

When examining the extravagant vocabulary of Augusto dos Anjos and the unique function of these often hazy structures in the eyes of the reader—due to their musicality and the overall composition of the verse—we must also consider the outcome of the constructions that utilize such words: what we refer to as verbal iconography. To evoke the seemingly infinite suffering of nature—even that which is voiceless, such as plants and vegetation—the poet employs the striking image of a "profound forest organism" in the poem "The Forest." This image, as sophisticated as it is evocative, unfolds through the dynamism of the versification employed:

> There's in this world a routed vim!
> Every profound forest organism
> Is living pain, locked in a disguise...
>
> Only coarse elements in it remain,
> —Ambitions which trunks became,
> For never could they be realized!

The image thus becomes a tangible representation of pain within a specific collective that, in fact, struggles to articulate its experiences in words. It resembles a narrative, achieved through the sophisticated use of imagery evoked by rhetorical devices, particularly metaphor and metonymy.

This type of composition renders the poems made by Augusto dos Anjos akin to fragments of unknown paintings by Hieronymus Bosch, as they strive to *graphically depict* (often gruesome) abstract concepts. Similar to the Platonic example mentioned at the beginning of this text, Anjos seeks to evoke an almost sensual aspect of the horror associated with the flesh, thereby making his ideas tangible for the reader. This process is evident in one of the author's most lauded poems, "Soliloquy of a Visionary." The very first verse is a great example about imagery: a dark sacrifice aimed at unraveling the "old and metaphysical Mystery":

Like an Anatomy Lesson

> So as to deflower the labyrinth
> Of the old and metaphysical Mystery,
> I ate my crude eyes at the cemetery,
> An anthropophagus famished in't!

Finally, it's time to see in detail the *meanings* evoked by such unique poetry. For the author, Augusto dos Anjos, the issue was quite simple and direct: the presentation, through poetic form, of a materialist philosophical conception, accompanied by distinct interpretations of certain philosophical ideas typical of the 19th and 20th centuries. Evidently, these concepts were not new within the context of Brazilian thought; in the 1880s, Rui Barbosa had already expressed opinions on the importance of science in education, clearly reflecting the influence of Herbert Spencer's ideas (see Gatti Junior and Santos). In the 1870s, Tobias Barreto introduced the Brazilian public to philosophical reflections inspired by Social Darwinism and Haeckel's Monism. Through Positivism, various strands of materialism were imported and gradually integrated into philosophy courses throughout Brazil—perhaps this was even the origin of philosophical obsessions in Augusto dos Anjos' poetry. However, as noted in the passage from Plato at the beginning of this brief essay, the imagery and linguistic construction of Anjos' poems are so memorable that they transform the ideas associated with them and the meanings of each verse, often surpassing their original intentions. The concepts evoked by Augusto dos Anjos thus gain a dizzying momentum through the powerful imagery of his language, contrasting with the formal rigor of the poetic structure he employed. This hallucinatory musicality is crafted through an array of unusual vocabulary elements, characterized by a unique exoticism stemming from their scientific origins. The fascination that these contradictory intersections evoke in the Brazilian reader is considerable.

III. Remote and Near Fragments

From a broad perspective, the funereal (or fatalistic) theme and philosophical approach of Augusto de Anjos can be traced back to a distant ancestor: the Graveyard Poetry of the 18th century. In this genre, pre-Romantic English poets such as Thomas Gray and Edward Young expressed their somber verses. Objectively, the primary precursor to the poems in the book *Eu* was Charles Baudelaire. His renowned work, *Les Fleurs du Mal*, published in 1857, quickly became embroiled in intense controversy. The book was banned due to its immoral and irreligious content, and its circulation was contingent upon the suppression of six poems. Even prior to its official release, Baudelaire had published several poems under the same title, *Les Fleurs du Mal*, in 1855 in the *Revue des Deux Mondes*. This earlier publication faced vehement criticism from the newspaper *Le Figaro*, which condemned the poetry as "poésie de charnier et d'abattoir" ["graveyard and slaughterhouse poetry"] (Resende and Anjos 158-159). The author of this indictment, deputy prosecutor Ernest Pinard, specifically targeted poems that clearly subverted moral values, evoking a sense of horror through powerful imagery, as exemplified in one of the banned poems, "The Metamorphoses of the Vampire":

> When she had drained the marrow out of all my bones,
> When I turned listlessly amid my languid moans,
> To give a kiss of love, nothing was with me but
> A greasy leather flask that overflowed with pus!
> (Baudelaire 255)

These images of the human body (and all things) in states of decay and decline, so bizarre to the poetry of Baudelaire's era—whether influenced by Classicism or Romanticism—were intertwined with erotic undertones and profound philosophical speculations that would shape the emergence of Symbolist Art. Baudelaire's poetic creations were all structured within a rigorous yet highly melodic poetic form, and his influences included the visionary theology by Emanuel Swedenborg and the stark philosophy of the Marquis de Sade. In this manner, Baudelaire expanded the horizons for several visionaries who would soon emerge in a context of burgeoning Symbolist and Decadent experimentation. Among this illustrious brotherhood was Augusto dos Anjos, alongside other members such as the poets of German Expressionism—most notably during its early years, from 1905 to 1914—like Gottfried Benn and Georg Heym. The pioneering poets of Expressionism, such as Augusto dos Anjos, chose to explore representations of the decaying body and decay itself, both in poetry and prose. A certain apocalyptic perspective, influenced by the specter of war, imbued Expressionism with a fatalistic fervor and a fascinated pessimism regarding the world—elements that resonate with the work of Augusto dos Anjos. In his debut poetry collection, *Morgue* (1912), released the same year as *Eu*, Gottfried Benn presents grim scenes in a morgue, as exemplified in the poem "Lovely Childhood": "The mouth of a girl who had long lain among the reeds looked gnawed away./ As the breast was cut open, the gullet showed full of holes" (Benn 213). Sharing a similar obsession with autopsies and the often repulsive activities associated with morgues, Georg Heym composed a brief report, almost resembling a prose poem, titled "The Autopsy." In this work, even amidst the brutal and commonplace fate of human bodies on dissection tables, a lyrical space can still be found. Therefore, it is not difficult to recognize a thematic, formal, and conceptual solidarity among these authors and within German Expressionism as a whole, with Augusto dos Anjos' visions, even if this kind of brotherhood between the Brazilian outsider and the German band of misfits never fully materialized in concrete terms.

And so, we return to Brazil, the homeland of Augusto dos Anjos, who endeavored to position his complex poetry within an intermediate space between local avant-garde movements and a past that critics long regarded as little more than a footnote in literary history. In this context, Augusto dos Anjos could only be recognized as a great poet by neutralizing—as João Adolfo Hansen reminds us, quoting the critic and poet Ferreira Gullar— the notion that he was merely an adherent of "a complicated rhetoric or pedantic verbalism of an adolescent who has read too much Spencer, Haeckel, and Schopenhauer." This may explain why there have been no followers or heirs to Augusto dos

Anjos' style: his language continues to provoke controversy even among researchers, scholars, and critics, necessitating some form of justification. Perhaps a potential disciple is the singular, eccentric, and kitsch figure, 'Count Belamorte,' the pseudonym of Joviano Martins Soares Filho, who penned the following verses, collected in his book *A Dança dos Espectros* [*The Wraith's Dance*], published in 1963:

> Verme, entre nós que diferença existe?
> Nenhuma! O homem — produto da cobiça —
> A tentação da carne não resiste,
> E tu, vives somente de carniça![*]

Although the philosophical essence of Augusto dos Anjos is minimally present in the verses of 'Conde Belamorte,' some of the strange resonances of his dark and morbid obsessions endure. Augusto dos Anjos and his heritage remains—despite being lauded in every conceivable context—unfathomable, like something that seems to evade categorization, vanishing into an extraordinary horizon of events. As described by Hansen and other critics, his poetry could be seen as a watchtower of an impregnable fortress—thus avoided by many, yet captivating like the enigma of the Sphinx.

Alcebiades Diniz Miguel

---

[*] "Worm, betwixt us hat difference exists?/ None! Man—a product of avarice—/ The temptation of the flesh doesn't resist,/ And you, solely on carrion you live!" (translation by Maurício Búrigo). See Conde Belamorte 154.

Works Cited

Baudelaire, Charles. *The Flowers of Evil*. Translated by James McGowan. Oxford: Oxford University Press, 1998.

Benn, Gottfried. *Primal Vision: Selected Writings of Gottfried Benn*. Ed. E. B. Ashton. New York: New Directions, 1971.

Conde Belamorte. *A Dança dos Espectros*. Belo Horizonte: Gráfica Serrana, 1963.

Gatti Júnior Décio and Leonardo Batista dos Santos. "Ciência, evolução e educação em Herbert Spencer." *Estudos avançados* 36: 105 (May 2022), 305-320. https://doi.org/10.1590/s0103-4014.2022.36105.018.

Hansen, João Adolfo. "*Eu*, semelhante a um cachorro de atalaia." Augusto dos Anjos. *Eu: fac-símile da edição do autor de 1912*. São Paulo: Edições Narval, 2023.

Plato. *The Republic*. Translation by Paul Shorey. Cambridge, Massachusetts and London: Harvard University Press and William Heinemann, 1978.

Resende, Letícia Campos de and Yuri Cerqueira dos Anjos. "O processo contra *As Flores do Mal* (1857): sustentação oral do procurador Ernest Pinard." *Non Plus*, 6: 12 (2017), 157-168.

CHRONOLOGY

1881

Realism (1881-1902) begins in Brazil, with the publication of *Memórias póstumas de Brás Cubas*, by Machado de Assis ~ Naturalism (1881-1902), likewise, with *O Mulato*, by Aluísio Azevedo. (These and the subsequent literary movements in Brazil follow, with a certain delay, the French previous, though still contemporary, ones.)

1882

Parnassianism (1882-1893) begins in Brazil, with the publication of *Fanfarras*, by Teófilo Dias; together with Symbolism (see below), it was a major influence in dos Anjos' early poems ~ 19 April: Charles Darwin (b. 1809), English evolutionary theorist and author of *On the Origin of Species* (1859), dies with symptoms of ischemic heart disease and cardiac failure.

1883

13 February: Richard Wagner (b. 1813), German composer of the opera *Tristan und Isolde* (1859), dies of a heart attack.

1884

20 April: Augusto de Carvalho Rodrigues dos Anjos is born at the Engenho de Pau d'Arco, a sugarcane mill and plantation, in Cruz do Espírito Santo, State of Paraíba. He is the third child of Alexandre Rodrigues dos Anjos and D. Córdula de Carvalho Rodrigues dos Anjos. At the same engenho he gets his first letters and secondary education from his father.

1886

19 July: Cesário Verde (b. 1855), Portuguese poet whose works were posthumously compiled in *O Livro de Cesário Verde* (1901), and an undeniable influence over dos Anjos, dies of tuberculosis.

Chronology

1887

Santiago Ramón y Cajal (1852-1934), Spanish neuroscientist, starts to investigate the central nervous system and demonstrates the discontinuity and individuality of nervous cells, leading to the neuron doctrine, considered the foundation of modern neuroscience.

1888

13 May: Abolition of Slavery in Brazil (the last country in the world to abolish it).

1889

15 November: Proclamation of the Republic in Brazil, by a military coup which ended a constitutional monarchy (Empire of Brazil) of 67 years.

1893

Symbolism (-1902) begins in Brazil, with the publication of *Missal* and *Broquéis*, by Cruz e Sousa. Together with Parnassianism, it was a major influence on dos Anjos' early poems.

1894

Ernst Haeckel (1834-1919), German biologist, theorist of Monism, publishes the first volume of his *Systematische Phylogenie* (second and third volume in 1895-1896), refining and expanding upon his development of evolutionary theory and exploration of the relationships between organisms from his seminal work *Generelle Morphologie der Organismen* (1866).

1895

8 November: Wilhelm Conrad Röntgen (1845-1923), German physicist, discovers a new type of electromagnetic radiation he temporarily terms X-ray. (A year later the first X-ray photograph is taken.)

1898

21 April-13 August: Spanish-American War ~ Martinus Beijerinck (1851-1931), Dutch microbiologist, after replicating the experiments of Dmitri Ivanovsky (1864-1920), Russian botanist, who had described an extremely minuscule infectious agent (1892), names the new pathogen *virus*.

1900

Dos Anjos takes preparatory exams for the Lyceu Parahybano, in João Pessoa, capital city of Paraíba ~ His first poem, certainly composed in the previous year, the sonnet "Saudade," appears in the *Almanaque do Estado da Paraíba* ~ He frequently travels to the capital, relating to the local intelligentsia ~ 25 August: Friedrich Nietzsche (b. 1844), German philosopher and author of *Also sprach Zarathustra* (1883), dies of pneumonia, after a stroke.

1901

17 January: Dos Anjos publishes the sonnet "Abandonada" in the newspaper *O Comércio*, starting an assiduous collaboration which will last until 1907 ~ 31 July: He publishes the sonnet "A Pecadora," giving rise to a polemic with an anonymous critic, as expressed in his "Carta Aberta" of the 20th of August.

1903

February: Dos Anjos moves to Recife, capital city of the State of Pernambuco, where he is enrolls in the Law School ~ 19 August: He publishes "Idealizações" in *O Comércio* ~ 8 December: Herbert Spencer (b. 1820), English philosopher and author of *A System of Synthetic Philosophy* (1862), dies of poor health due to old age.

1904

2 January: Dos Anjos publishes the sonnet "Vandalismo" in *O Comércio*, along with various other poems during the year.

1905

13 January: Death of dos Anjos' father. Six days later, he publishes in *O Comércio* three sonnets in memory of the deceased, though

describing rather his last agonies and postmortem state ~ 12 October: He starts the "Crônica paudarquense," in prose, in the same newspaper, besides engaging in two polemics.

1906

He is enrolled in the fourth year of Law School ~ From July to September, he publishes two long poems, "Queixas Noturnas" and "Poema Negro," as well as the sonnet "Versos Íntimos," all in *O Comércio*.

1907

In July, he publishes one long poem, "Tristezas de Um Quarto Minguante,", and the sonnet *"Ricordanza della Mia Gioventù,"* in *O Comércio* ~ 2 December: He concludes his studies at the Law School.

1908

He moves to Parahyba do Norte (today, João Pessoa), the capital of the state of Paraíba, where he gives private lessons ~ He collaborates with the newspaper *Nonevar* ~ 4 August: He publishes the long poem "As Cismas do Destino," in the review *Terra Natal*, with great repercussion ~ 9 October: Death of his mother's stepfather and family patriarch, Aprígio Pessoa Melo, which leaves the Engenho de Pau d'Arco in grave financial situation ~ He teaches at the Instituto Maciel Pinheiro ~ Betrothed since September, he gets close to João Machado, the new governor of Paraíba, and is nominated as teacher at the Lyceu Parahybano.

1909

He starts to collaborate with the newspaper *A União*, in which he publishes the sonnet "Budismo Moderno" and numerous poems during the year ~ He delivers an address on the 13th of May (Abolition of Slavery), shocking the audience with his incomprehensible and bizarre lexicon ~ He abandons the Instituto Maciel Pinheiro.

1910

1 April: He publishes a long poem, "Mistérios de um Fósforo," followed by another, "Noite de um Visionário," in *A União* ~ 4 July: He marries Ester Fialho ~ He continues his collaboration

with *Nonevar* ~ His family sells the Engenho de Pau d'Arco ~ Unable to get a teaching degree, he resigns from the Lyceu Parahybano ~ 6 September: He embarks with his wife on the packet *Acre*, destined for Rio de Janeiro, arriving on the 13th of the same month. They lodge at a boarding-house on Largo do Machado, and then move to Avenida Central. He cannot find employment until the end of the year ~ The term 'expressionism' likely coined by Antonin Matějček; the movements includes poets such as Georg Trakl, Gottfried Benn and Georg Heym, all of whom, though probably unknown to dos Anjos, had a kinship with his clinical-scientific terminology, crude descriptions, and predilection for such motifs as decay and putrefaction.

1911

2 January: Ester, in her sixth month of pregnancy, loses the couple's first baby, for whom dos Anjos writes a sonnet a month later ~ He is nominated as teacher of Geography, Chorography and Cosmography at the Ginásio Nacional (today, Colégio Pedro II) ~ 23 November: Their daughter Glória is born ~ They constantly move to different residences.

1912

He collaborates with the newspaper *O Estado*, besides giving lessons at the Escola Normal (today, Instituto de Educação Professor Ismael Coutinho) ~ 6 July: The printing of *Eu* is finished (with a run of 1,000 copies); the cost of 500,000 reis is covered by dos Anjos and his brother Odilon ~ The publication of *Eu* leaves a great impression (and a sense of an estrangement) on literary critics, who oscillate between enthusiasm and repulsion.

1913

12 June: Dos Anjos' son Guilherme Augusto is born ~ He continues to teach in various establishments ~ The book *Perfis do Norte*, by Santos Netto, a collection of biographies of personalities from the north of Brazil (with a chapter dedicated to dos Anjos), is published.

Chronology

1914

26 April: He publishes the sonnet "O Lamento das Coisas" in the newspaper *Gazeta de Leopoldina*, directed by the husband of a sister-in-law, Rômulo Pacheco ~ 1 July: He is nominated director of the Grupo Escolar Ribeiro Junqueira (today, Escola Municipal Ribeiro Junqueira), in Leopoldina, a city in Minas Gerais, to where he moves by the end of the month ~ 28 July: World War I begins ~ 12 November: Ill since the 30th of October, he expires at four o'clock in the morning, of pneumonia.

1920

With the title *Eu (Poesias, completas)*, edited and prefaced by Órris Soares, the second edition of his book is published by the Imprensa Oficial da Paraíba.

1928

With the addition of 46 unpublished poems and with the title *Eu, e outras poesias*, a third edition is launched by the Livraria Castilho from Rio de Janeiro, becoming an extraordinary public and critical success.

Translator's Note

When I began to write poetry in my mid-adolescence (long before I became a translator…), Augusto dos Anjos was the first Brazilian poet to arouse my interest and to have a strong influence over my initiation, so much so that I started writing a number of rather imitative sonnets or short rhymed poems, both in his style and with the same pessimistic temperament… I was soon to quit writing sonnets and end rhymed poems for good, but in spite of the somewhat loose meter in most of them, it was nevertheless surely a good exercise for poetic devices and my own sense of rhythm.

When time came for the conception of this project, Augusto dos Anjos was an obvious choice, although I also considered other poets. As an unprecedented translation whose publication would serve as an introduction to the work of the poet in an English-speaking sphere, and with some limitation concerning the length of the book, I decided on a selection of sonnets and a few longer poems from the third edition (*Eu, e outras poesias*, 1928) of the first and only work published in his life, the *Eu* (1912), with the addition of the so-called 'other poems,' comprising ones probably, or mostly, written after 1910 and until the year of his death. I did not select the poems beforehand, but rather began to translate some sonnets that were my personal favorites as well as others that were notorious with the public and the critics, then proceeded to reread and choose others which had failed my recollection or were somewhat 'novel' to me, considering the specific approach and renewed attention necessary to render them into English and compose a book, and still any poems which I had never read before. Of course, the poems selected here are not 'final' as part of a definitive, comprehensive compilation, but are entirely my own as 'finds.' While I was working out their translation and becoming increasingly familiarized and at ease with their language, style, and other concerns involved in reaching a 'voice' for the poet in English, I ceased to worry about the fortuity and partiality of my choices, and now think that it is useless to justify the outcome, though this should not be regarded as an excuse. As I mentioned above, as an introduction to the work of Augusto dos Anjos, the selection is a reasonable one, encompassing early sonnets, included in *Eu* and perhaps the 'other poems;' sonnets of the poet's maturity which constitute the core of the first edition, as well as two of his most significant longer poems from it; and the late sonnets and one long poem, both from the 'other poems.' (Strictly speaking, 14 sonnets and 2 longer poems from *Eu*, and 10 sonnets and 1 long poem from the 'other poems.')

As regards the translation of the poems, having first decided to maintain their content as accurate as possible, and to keep their rhyme scheme, I left the meter to be handled throughout the process, thinking that the abundance of monosyllabic words in English would help me in the free play and countless possibilities of arranging the verses, both creatively and rhythmically, which proved right—to a certain point, at least. In the meanwhile, I was reading some criticism on dos Anjos' poetry and work, and found this analysis by Ferreira Gullar, Brazilian poet and critic, in his study "Augusto dos Anjos or Northeastern Life and Death," which reads:

> At the simple reading of the poems one realizes that this poet was not a chiseler of verses, an exigent craftsman. In his poetry, the determinant is the content, to which he eagerly gives form, sometimes magisterially, thanks to a profound intuition of the form and a very high verbal virtuosity. His poems present here and there the consequences of this eagerness: verses now too hard, now too loose, excess of adjectivation, forced rhymes . . . that perfection never appears as result of formal preoccupation

or of posterior polishing work, but actually as reflex of an inner state which achieves full poetic formulation. (Gullar 49)[*]

This analysis came to strengthen my resolution, since I myself had reached a similar conclusion before, to deal with the meter as freely and loosely as I had been doing, so as to compromise the least content, the rhymes being the first element of the verse to be set.

So, by just following the rhyme scheme of the original poems—predominantly *abba/abba/ccd/eed* in the sonnets, with variations in the octaves (*abba/baab*; *abab/abab*; *abab/baba*) and sestets (*cde/cde*; *cdc/ede*) for the rest, with no regular scheme on the whole, rather combinations of one of the former with one of the latter (in "Suprême Convulsion," the *ccd/eed* scheme of the original was changed by *ccd/dee* in the translation); with *aabccb* in "Monologue of a Shadow;" *abba* for "The Misgivings of Destiny" in each stanza; and "At a Forge" with no scheme at all—, I started picking and translating words, some kept from the original rhymes, some perceived from amid the very verse, or from the previous or the next one, resulting in inversions of sentences or enjambments, new words inserted, others transposed or replaced by synonyms words or phrases, with verb tenses changed or verbs in the active voice used in the passive, multi-word verbs split, adverbs added to fit the meaning, intensifiers attached to adjectives, postpositional adjectives, clauses rewritten, and so forth, anything that could fit, with only a vague idea of the final verse translation with such adaptations which would be necessary afterwards, the intricacies of which I shall talk about later. It was a most demanding labor, to set my mind on handling all sorts of possibilities, with the octaves in particular, having two times four rhymes to 'find' at the same time, in a brainstorming trance which at times took hours. With the sestets and strophes of the longer poems, which could be dealt by couplets, the task was comparably easier, as far as the number

---

[*] This and subsequent quotes are in my translation.

Translator's Note

of rhymes to be simultaneously set is concerned. Also easier to set into the scheme were the original rhymes with nouns, adjectives or adverbs with the same repeated suffix, as well as present or past participles with their common desinence, among others, which recurred in the entire strophe or octave; sometimes the translation itself, either faithful to the original or according to the words I had picked here and there so as to keep any rhyme scheme afforded me an easy way. Therefore, the translation had its first step with a list of end rhymes, for each sonnet a complete one, for the longer poems one by strophe, before going to the next step, the building of the verses themselves. But before that, I shall speak of the types of rhymes which I came up with.

Though I managed to achieve a fairly great amount of perfect rhymes or, at least, nearly-perfect ones, such as assonant, identical (*rimes riches*), light, syllabic, or wrenched rhymes, sometimes making use of neologisms, archaisms, obsolete words, words borrowed mostly from Latin or French, scientific jargon, etc. (not necessarily coincidental with the original rhymes or any words picked from the verses to supply a rhyme, but nevertheless in accordance with the poet's own use and style), other times adding words of my own that were somewhat slightly redundant or reinforced the meaning of the sentence, I couldn't help indulging myself (out of exhaustion of resources, or creativity, perhaps…) in the use of plenty of imperfect rhymes and others, rather more scarcely appearing, such as eye, forced, identical, light, or sight rhymes. Naturally most of these didn't come up intentionally, unless by my own propensity toward vocalic sounds, although, likewise with the loose meter, I left aside a number of times a rigorous consideration of the stressed syllables, making light or wrenched rhymes. Thus, there is a variety of extravagant, exotic, peculiar, if not just merely poor rhymes, as one might say, which nevertheless work phonetically and melodically. Here are three short samples (quite abundant themselves, albeit comprising less than half of the non-perfect rhymes used) taken from the longer poems, of the most conspicuous of these *ugly beauties*: aloft/

know not; residues/woods; plebeian/ideas; outworn/horror; reminds of/shows off; halo/him so; efforts/remorses; spent/damned; canvases/incestuousness; dismays/bloodstains; lantern/torments; there is/reappears; grief/deep; converts/earth; science/essence; suicidal/lives |-īvz| all; whirlwind/thundering; pierce/photospheres; etc. (in "Monologue of a Shadow," p. 3-17);[*] *Bridge/sieged; vault/bald; enormous/rhinoceros; beastly/buildings; hounds/mouths; lewd/loose; globes/unfolded; hues/fetuses; apriorism/antrum; cloth/shot; worlds/hold; for sure/capture; sapiens/bent; thus/viscus; mind/knife; enter/end; disfigured/seizure; tussis/phthisis; dense/race; stone/thrown; miserable/little; bedew/you; touch/earth; Vinci/lynx; freed/figures; stench/bent; maleficent/bang; goblins/noising; gathered/shelter; acts/incests; jaundice/pubicity; spy me/hypnotize me; so/embryos; miniature/minute; forth/sloth; inverts/inert; secret/complete; lesson/reason; peaks/sheaves; binds them/Carolingian; species/seas; peace/plead; burns/fun; strangled/toad; fool/full; into/goo; went/strength; thus/dunces; name it/famine; acquiesces/milkless; such so/puddles; cathedrals/skulls; lack/masks; souse/stout; assassin/Destiny; endless/recesses; universal/parcel; Idea/nymphaea; horrid/symbolic; stirs/myrrh; whins/slaughtering; spots/tops; obfuscate/takes; mean/paraselene; tremble/poles; angst/gland; psychoplasm/asthma; mutter/butchers'; betwixt/conceit; juices/lunies; creatures/uterus; plead/Archimedes; mark/anasarca; towel/pestilential; funest/forest; display/disarray; maledict/scripts; insurrected/Pandects; together/cadavers; came/complains; resigned/lied; labor/failure; but/moribund; hell/eternal;* etc. (in "The Misgivings of Destiny," p. 27-63); *prisoner/embers; today/laid/away; fulgid/horrid; descended/condemned/then; species/proceeds; creaking/hearing/cling/reacting; unnerved/crushed/jerked/punished; each/screech; was/warm; synergy/sickly; suns/clung; trismus/paroxysms/abysms; fears/fingers; vengeful/dull; gruesome/antiphon; crescendo/horrendous; convulsing/being/margins;* etc. (in "At a Forge," p. 97-103). I could go on indefinitely with a rather long list, and also with those from the sonnets, but they are to be found in the translated poems themselves. Instead, I would rather present, then, three sonnets which comprehend either perfect (some achieved by the artifice of making use of neologisms, archaisms, etc., as I mentioned above) or nearly-perfect and imperfect rhymes (and others):

---

[*] This and subsequent page references are to the present edition.

Translator's Note

Martyrdom of the Artist

Ingrate Art! And albeit, <u>despondent</u>[1],
His eye ellipsoidal orbit burn as it may,
To exteriorize the thought he's <u>intent</u>[1],
That which in his frontal cells he stays.

Delayed is the Idea! Inspiration delays!
Here trembling, tears the paper, <u>violent</u>[2],
As the soldier who his uniform tore away
In the desperation of the last <u>moment</u>[2]!

Tries to weep and dry his eyes linger!...
He's like the paralytic who, for lack
Of his own voice and in the raging hot

Fever to speak in vain, with brute fingers
To speak, his tongue pulls and pulls back,
And to his mouth even a word comes not!

([1]despondent/intent; [2]violent/moment: syllabic rhymes)

("O Martírio do Artista"/"Martyrdom of the Artist," p. 75)

Psychology of a Loser

I, son of carbon and of <u>ammoniac</u>[1],
Monster of obscurity and <u>rutilance</u>[2],
Suffer, since the epigenesis of <u>infance</u>[2],
The evil influence of the signs of <u>zodiac</u>[1].

Most profoundly hypochondriac,
This ambient arouses my repugnance…
Up my mouth comes an urge as urgence
Escaping from the mouth of a cardiac.

Now the worm — laborer of the <u>ruins</u>[3] —,
The rotten blood of carnage <u>devouring</u>[3],
And declaring war to life all around,

Is spying my eyes so as to gnaw them[4],
And shall leave me only my hair, then[4],
In the inorganic coldness of the ground!

([1]ammoniac (neologism)/zodiac: perfect rhyme; [2]rutilance (rare noun)/infance (obsolete noun): syllabic rhyme; [3]ruins/devouring: imperfect rhyme; [4]them/then: assonant rhyme)

("Psicologia de um Vencido"/"Psychology of a Loser," p. 21)

The Idea

Whence does it come? From whatever[1]
Crude matter comes this light falling sur[2]
Nebulae of unknown crypts, mysterious[2],
Like the stalactites inside a cavern[1]?

Comes from the psychogenetic and stern[3]
Battle of a fascicle of molecules nervous
Which, in disintegrations marvelous,
Deliberates, and then wants and exerts[3]!

From the absconse encephalon constringing it[4],
To arrive, after, at the cords of the larynx[4],
Phthisic, tenuous, minimal, rachitic...

Breaks the centripetal force to which is tied[5],
But suddenly, and almost dead, it collides[5]
With the tatter of a tongue paralytic!

([1]whatever/cavern; [2]sur/mysterious; [3]stern/exerts; [4]constringing it/larynx; [5]tied/collides: imperfect rhymes)

("A Idéia"/"The Idea," p. 23)

Before approaching the building of the verses and afterwards the poems within their translation, I shall quote some significant considerations, again by Ferreira Gullar, on the incipient modern poetry in Brazil in the early twentieth century—culminating in Modernism in 1922, of which Augusto dos Anjos is one of the precursors—and on the poet's expedient in attaining an original and unique style within that context.

> The rupture with the former view—and with former forms—wasn't made in a trice, but at the end of attempts, by feeling one's way, and through contradictory pursuits . . . attempts to, so to speak, ignore the prosaic reality. But . . . already perceived, mingled with the yearning to flee from the prosaic world, is prosaicness. And when the language of poetry, divesting itself of its golden plumage, lowered to the level of prose, then the very poet lowered to the ground . . . decided to inhabit the quotidian . . . . [I]n all of them [the poets] the language stripped itself of the old rhetoric, the concrete experience of life became the matter of poetry: the poet started to speak from then on with the common speech. (Gullar 30)

> Poetry is, therefore, a deliberately perplexing discourse, which in one way or another is contrary to the normality of discourse. The poet doesn't want to digress about objects, doesn't want his language to be mere reference to the world: he wants the poem to be the place where experience occurs—deflagrated—concretely. In order to achieve that, the modern poet makes use of a series of resources which constitute the characteristics of his new language: inusitate syntactic construction, rupture of the spontaneous rhythm of language, shock of words, montage of words and images, chaotic enumeration, mixture of colloquial and erudite verbal forms, of vulgar words with 'poetic' words, etc. Some of these resources were used by Augusto dos Anjos. (32)

And as regards the poet's peculiar vocabulary and poetic innovation, Gullar writes:

> How is Augusto dos Anjos's novelty occult in his poetry? By effect of the same radical attitude which, making him break with the verbal and social conveniences of

poetry, led him to dispute the poetic over the putridity of cemeteries and the vulgarity of brothels, to mingle beauty and disgust and, as a sort of defense, to arm himself with a 'scientific,' prestigious vocabulary, which imposes upon his language the seal of the period and threatens to 'date' it. Thus, the novelty which there is in his poetry makes way amidst that amalgam of vulgarity and bad taste which is, notwithstanding, an indispensable condition in order that, in this case, the novelty be produced. Because, as we have stated before, the poetry of August dos Anjos isn't born from a critical assimilation and gradual exceeding of poetic techniques and values, but from a conjunction of factors which oblige him to break with the poetic language ([and] with the view) in vogue. (29)

Then, summarizing it with the poet's particular style: "Augusto, in spite of the scientistic or rationalizing appearance of his poems, is above all a creator of 'atmospheres,' in this lying, perhaps, the main force of his 'gothic' and theatrical language" (49).

I've already spoken of all demands implied and artifices I had to use due to the picking of rhymes. Most of the 'juggling' (inversions of sentences and other intricate solutions) which followed was determined by that, some of it didn't depend on the rhymes, and many "inusitate syntactic constructions" were from the poet's own pen, which were or were not kept. As regards the scientific vocabulary, that was not much of a problem, since it almost entirely derives from Greek and Latin, and remains similar in both Portuguese and English (practically all of it translated faithfully, unless I opted for a common synonym to make a rhyme or used a scientific one—where in the original there was not—with entry in dictionaries), as well as the "erudite verbal forms" (comprising also the use of archaisms, obsolete words, etc.), neologisms (created by the author or by myself), and so forth. (I made notes on those for which I considered indispensable an indication or elucidation.) Nor was the translation of "colloquial" and "vulgar" words an issue, as this did not imply, on my part, any modernization to a current language usage, and since their "shock" or contrast with the "poetic" ones was intentional. The punctuation mostly respected the original, with few, slight changes (added or suppressed commas, semi-colons, dashes, etc.) only for the purpose of clarification of meaning.

Now I present some excerpts taken from the longer poems and others from some of the sonnets, in both the original and the translation, with an indication of my translating procedures (which, for readers not proficient in Portuguese, may help at least in realizing the intricacies involved):

> Disse isto a Sombra. E, <u>ouvindo estes vocábulos</u>[1],
> <u>Da luz da lua</u>[2] aos pálidos venábulos,
> <u>Na ânsia de</u>[3] um nervosíssimo entusiasmo,
> <u>Julgava ouvir monótonas corujas</u>[4],
> <u>Executando, entre caveiras sujas</u>[5],
> A orquestra arrepiadora do sarcasmo!

Said so the Shadow. And <u>as I did hear
Such words</u>[1], in <u>moonlight's</u>[2] pale spears,
<u>Anxious of</u>[3] a most nervous enthusiasm,
<u>Monotone owls I guess I was hearing</u>[4],
<u>In the midst of dirty skulls, executing</u>[5]
The terrifying orchestra of sarcasm

([1] enjambment: hear/such words; [2]transposition: moonlight's—genitive, *orig.* postmodifier; [3]transposition: anxious of—adjective phrase, *orig.* prepositional phrase; [4]inversion; [5]inversion)

> <u>E o turbilhão de tais fonemas acres</u>[1]
> <u>Trovejando grandíloquos massacres</u>[2],
> <u>Há de ferir-me as auditivas portas</u>[3],
> Até que <u>minha</u>[4] efêmera cabeça
> Reverta à quietação da treva espessa
> E à palidez das fotosferas mortas!

<u>And such acrid phonemes' whirlwind</u>[1]
<u>Grandiloquent massacres thundering</u>[2],

<u>My auditive doors shall then pierce</u>³,
Until this ephemeral head of <u>mine</u>⁴
Revert to the quiet of the thick night
And the pallor of dead photospheres!

(¹inversion; ²inversion; ³inversion; ⁴transposition: mine—possessive pronoun, *orig.* possessive adjective)

(in "Monólogo de uma Sombra/Monologue of a Shadow," p. 16-17, str. 29, 31)

> Na austera abóbada alta <u>o fósforo alvo</u>
> <u>Das estrelas luzia</u>¹... O calçamento
> Sáxeo, de asfalto rijo, atro e vidrento,
> Copiava a polidez de um <u>crânio calvo</u>².

<u>The stars</u>, in the austere high vault,
<u>Shone phosphorous white</u>¹... A petrous
Paving, of rigid asphalt, dark, vitreous,
Copied the polish of a <u>cranium bald</u>².

(¹tranposition: the stars—subject, *orig.* qualifier; phosphorous white—predicative, *orig.* subject; ²postposition)

> Tal uma horda feroz de cães famintos,
> <u>Atravessando uma estação deserta</u>¹,
> <u>Uivava dentro do *eu*, com a boca aberta,</u>
> <u>A matilha espantada dos instintos</u>²!

As a feral horde of famished hounds,
<u>Through a desert station crossing</u>¹,
<u>The aghast pack of instincts howling</u>
<u>Was inside the *self*, with open mouths</u>²!

(¹inversion; ²reversion: *orig.* inverted sentence; transposition: howling was—past continuous (inverted), *orig.* simple past; enjambment: howling/was)

> <u>Livres de microscópios e escalpelos</u>¹,
> <u>Dançavam, parodiando saraus cínicos</u>²,

Translator's Note

> Bilhões de *centrossomas* apolínicos
> Na câmara <u>promíscua</u>[4] do *vitellus*.

<u>From microscopes and scalpels free</u>[1],
<u>Parodying cynic soirées, danced</u>[2] <u>some</u>[3]
Billions of apollonic *centrosomes*
In the *vitellus* chamber <u>of promiscuity</u>[4]

([1]inversion; [2]inversion; [3]insertion; [4]transposition: of promiscuity—post modifier, *orig.* adjective)

> A vingança dos mundos astronômicos
> <u>Enviava à terra extraordinária faca</u>[1],
> <u>Posta</u>[2] em rija adesão de goma laca
> Sobre os meus elementos anatômicos.

The vengeance of astronomic worlds
<u>Down earth an extraordinary knife sent</u>[1],
<u>To take</u>, with lac wax rigid adherence,
Of all my anatomic elements <u>hold</u>[2].

([1]inversion; [2]transposition: to take . . . hold—infinitive (split), *orig.* past participle)

> <u>Nem terás no trabalho que tiveste</u>
> <u>A misericordiosa toalha amiga</u>[1],
> Que afaga os homens doentes de bexiga
> E enxuga, à noite, as <u>pústulas da peste</u>[2]!

<u>Nor have the merciful friendly towel,</u>
<u>In the toil you've had, you will</u>[1],
That caresses men with smallpox ill,
Dries at night <u>pustules pestilential</u>[2]!

([1]inversion; splitting: have . . . you will; [2]transposition: pestilential—adjective, *orig.* postmodifier; postposition)

(in "As Cismas do Destino/The Misgivings of Destiny," p. 27-31, I, str. 2, 5, 8, 13; p. 57-58, III, str. 95)

Maurício Búrigo

>Dentro, a cuspir escórias¹
>De fúlgida limalha²
>Dardejando centelhas transitórias³,
>No horror da metalúrgica batalha
>O ferro⁴ chiava e ria!

Inside, scoriae spitting¹
 Of filings fulgid²,
Transitory scintillations darting³,
The iron, in metallurgic battle, horrid⁴,
 Creaked and laughed away⁵!

(¹inversion; ²postposition; ³inversion; ⁴inversion; intercalation: in metallurgic battle, horrid; transposition: horrid—adjective, *orig.* prepositional phrase; ⁵insertion)

>Da qual, bruta, provinha
>Como de um negro cáspio de água impura¹
>>A multissecular desesperança
>>De sua espécie abjeta²
>Condenada a uma estática mesquinha³!

From which, brute, descended,
As if from impure water of Caspian blackness¹,
 Of its abject species
 The multisecular desperation²
To a measly static condemned³!

(¹transposition: impure water—noun phrase, *orig.* postmodifier; of Caspian blackness—postmodifier, *orig.* noun phrase; ²inversion; ³inversion)

>Era um cosmos inteiro sofredor¹,
>Cujo negror profundo
>>Astro nenhum exorna²
>>Gritando na bigorna³
>Asperamente a sua própria dor!

It was an entire cosmos suffering¹,
 Whose profound pitch-darkness

Translator's Note

<ins>Ornates not any one star</ins>²
<ins>On the anvil crying</ins>³, <ins>far</ins>⁴
Harshly, its <ins>very</ins>⁵ own hurting!

(¹transposition: suffering—participial adjective, *orig.* agent noun; ²inversion; ³inversion; ⁴insertion; ⁵insertion)

(in "Numa Forja/At a Forge," p. 96-99, str. 1, 2, 5)

<ins>Triste, a escutar, pancada por pancada</ins>¹,
A sucessividade dos segundos,
Ouço, <ins>em sons subterrâneos, do Orbe oriundos</ins>³,
O choro da Energia <ins>abandonada</ins>⁴!

<ins>Tap by tap, listening with sorrowfulness</ins>¹
To the successivity of the seconds <ins>round</ins>²,
I hear <ins>from the Orb, in subterranean sounds</ins>³,
The weep of Energy <ins>in its forsakenness</ins>⁴!

(¹inversion; transposition: with sorrowfulness—prepositional phrase, *orig.* adjective; ²insertion; ³inversion; suppression: from the Orb, *orig. lit.* 'originating' from the Orb; ⁴transposition: in its forsakenness—prepositional phrase, *orig.* participial adjective)

("O Lamento das Coisas/The Lament of Things," p. 85-86, str. 1)

<ins>Vestido de hidrogênio incandescente</ins>¹,
<ins>Vaguei um século, improficuamente</ins>²,
Pelas monotonias siderais…

<ins>Subi talvez</ins>³ às máximas alturas,
Mas, se hoje volto <ins>assim</ins>⁴, com a alma às escuras,
É necessário que ainda eu suba mais!

<ins>By incandescent hydrogen covered</ins>¹,
<ins>A century, unprofitably, as a rover,</ins>
Through sidereal monotonies <ins>I did go</ins>²…

Maurício Búrigo

To maximum heights <u>I may have climbed</u>[3],
But if now I'm back, my soul <u>thus</u>[4] blinded,
It's necessary that I climb yet more <u>so</u>[5]!

([1]inversion; [2]inversion; splitting: as a rover . . . I did go; transposition: to go as a rover—verb + prepositional phrase, *orig.* verb *lit.* 'to rover'; [3]transposition: I may have climbed—past modal structure, *orig.* verb + adverb *lit.* 'perhaps'; [4]shifting; [5]insertion)

("Solilóquio de um Visionário/Soliloquy of a Visionary," p. 70-71, str. 3, 4)

> Vês?! Ninguém assistiu ao formidável
> Enterro de tua última quimera.
> Somente a Ingratidão — <u>esta</u>[2] pantera —
> Foi tua companheira inseparável!
>
> Acostuma-te à lama que te espera!
> O Homem, que, nesta terra miserável,
> Mora entre feras, sente inevitável
> Necessidade de também <u>ser fera</u>[4].

See!? No one attended the formidable
Burial of your last chimaera <u>to spare</u>[1].
Only Ingratitude— a panther <u>there</u>[2]—
Was your companion, inseparable!

Be used to a mire that is your share!
Man, who, in this land <u>so</u>[3] miserable,
Lives among beasts, feels inevitable
Need to also <u>with a beast compare</u>[4].

([1]insertion; [2]transposition: there—adverb, *orig.* demonstrative adjective; [3]insertion; [4]inversion; transposition: with a beast—prepositional object, *orig.* predicative)

("Versos Íntimos/Intimate Verses," p. 80-81, str. 1, 2)

> <u>Começaste a existir, geléia crua</u>[1],
> E hás de crescer, no teu silêncio, <u>tanto</u>

Translator's Note

> Que, é natural, ainda algum dia, o pranto
> Das tuas concreções plásmicas flua²!

To exist, crude jelly, you're imbued¹,
And shall accrue, in silence, so might
Naturally the weeping, still sometime,
From your plasmic concretions issue²!

(¹inversion; intercalation: crude jelly; ²enjambment: might/ naturally; transposition: might issue—modal verb + infinitive, *orig.* present subjunctive; splitting: might . . . issue; shifting: still sometime, *orig.* intercalated between *lit.* 'is natural' and 'weeping')

("A Um Gérmen/To A Germ," p. 90-91, str. 1)

> Meia-noite. Ao meu quarto me recolho¹.
> Meu Deus! E este morcego! E, agora, vede:
> Na bruta ardência orgânica da sede,
> Morde-me a goela ígneo e escaldante molho.
>
> "Vou mandar levantar outra parede³..."
> — Digo. Ergo-me a tremer. Fecho o ferrolho
> E olho o teto. E vejo-o ainda, igual a um olho,
> Circularmente sobre a minha rede⁴!

Midnight. To recoil in my chamber I walk¹.
My God! And this bat! Now look, just²:
In the brute organic ardency of thirst,
Bites my gullet an igneous scalding stock.

"Have another wall built up, I must³..."
—I say. I raise trembling, bolt the lock,
Look at the ceiling. Over my hammock
I see it still, like an eye, circle headfirst⁴!

(¹inversion; insertion: I walk; ²insertion; ³inversion; insertion: I must; ⁴inversion; transposition: circle headfirst—adverb phrase, *orig.* adverb)

(O Morcego/The Bat, p. 18-19, str. 1, 2)

The dictionaries I used were old companions of mine which might make a fully equipped translator laugh at their supposed obsolescence. They are not so as regards the works of Augusto dos Anjos, and since I made no attempts to adapt his vocabulary, especially the colloquial and vulgar words so characteristic of him, alongside the other traits of his style they were blended with, to the modern speech, as before mentioned, the dictionaries served me well and right. The scientific and philosophical terms, though their definitions and theories might have become indeed obsolete, and the erudite and archaic words, are much the same as those of the poet's current times or are all somewhat atemporal, as far as the translation is concerned. I prevented myself from making exhausting notes on these terms and words, since they have all of them entries in dictionaries so far, a few times at least in a single one, the *Oxford English Dictionary* being anyone's last resort (problematic acceptions, obsolete words and neologisms are indicated in notes). But hardly ever did my own dictionaries fail me, and whether they did, it was nothing other ones 'at hand' for consultation wouldn't compensate; if even these, in turn, did not completely satisfy me, in any case they showed me the way. The actual time spent on those references went along with a train of thought triggered by the very first impasse or doubt. Otherwise it was intellectual hard work and creativity to find other acceptions that would fit an obfuscated meaning. Besides any obvious qualities a translator might or should have, one of the crucial ones is distrust—since one is fatefully a traitor, as the dictum goes—of words and the logic which composes them, in senses diverse and deceptive, either in the original or the target language… Nevertheless, the one and only dictionary of mine worth mentioning is the *Webster's Third New International Dictionary of the English Language, Unabridged* (1986 [1961]), an inestimable chest of treasure troves, both for my work in general and for this translation in particular, to which I am most grateful.

WORKS CITED

Gullar, Ferreira. "Augusto dos Anjos ou Vida e Morte Nordestina." Augusto dos Anjos. *Toda a Posia. Com un estudo crítico de Ferreira Gullar.* Rio de Janeiro: Paz e Terra, 1976. 13-59.

I/Eu
and other poems

Monólogo de uma Sombra

"Sou uma Sombra! Venho de outras eras,
Do cosmopolitismo das moneras...
Pólipo de recônditas reentrâncias,
Larva de caos telúrico, procedo
Da escuridão do cósmico segredo,
Da substância de todas as substâncias!

A simbiose das coisas me equilibra.
Em minha ignota mônada, ampla, vibra
A alma dos movimentos rotatórios...
E é de mim que decorrem, simultâneas,
A saúde das forças subterrâneas
E a morbidez dos seres ilusórios!

Pairando acima dos mundanos tetos,
Não conheço o acidente da *Senectus*
— Esta universitária sanguessuga
Que produz, sem dispêndio algum de vírus,
O amarelecimento do papirus
E a miséria anatômica da ruga!

Monologue of a Shadow

"I'm a Shadow! I come from other eras,
From the cosmopolitanism of moneras...
A polyp of recondite reentrances,
A larva of telluric chaos, I proceed
From the obscurity of cosmic secrecy,
From the substance of all substances!

By a symbiosis of things I'm equilibrated.
In my ignote, ample monad, vibrates
The soul of the rotatory motionings...
And from me derives, simultaneous,
The health of forces subterraneous
And the morbidity of illusory beings!

Over mundane roofs hovering aloft,
The accident of *Senectus*[*] I know not
— This universitarian[†] bloodsucker
Causing, with no waste of a virus,
The yellowing of the papyrus,
The anatomic misery of a pucker!

---

[*] Senectus *n.* Latin, 'senectitude,' 'old age;' also, *cap.* the Roman god of old age, equivalent to the Greek god Γῆρας (Geras).

[†] Universitarian *adj.* A double entendre: 'universalistic/ universitarian.'

Na existência social, possuo uma arma
— O metafisicismo de Abidarma —
E trago, sem bramânicas tesouras,
Como um dorso de azêmola passiva,
A solidariedade subjetiva
De todas as espécies sofredoras.

Com um pouco de saliva quotidiana
Mostro meu nojo à Natureza Humana.
A podridão me serve de Evangelho...
Amo o esterco, os resíduos ruins dos quiosques
E o animal inferior que urra nos bosques
É com certeza meu irmão mais velho!

Tal qual quem para o próprio túmulo olha,
Amarguradamente se me antolha,
À luz do americano plenilúnio,
Na alma crepuscular de minha raça
Como uma vocação para a Desgraça
E um tropismo ancestral para o Infortúnio.

Aí vem sujo, a coçar chagas plebéias,
Trazendo no deserto das ideias
O desespero endêmico do inferno,
Com a cara hirta, tatuada de fuligens
Esse mineiro doido das origens,
Que se chama o Filósofo Moderno!

Augusto dos Anjos - I

In social existence, a weapon I possess
— The Abhidharma's metaphysicalness[*] —
And without Brahmanic scissors I bring
— Dorsum of a beast of burden, passive —
The very solidarity rather subjective
Of the entirety of species suffering.

With a little saliva of the everyday
My disgust for Human Nature I lay.
As a Gospel serves me putridity...
I love manure, a privy's bad residues,
The low beast roaring in the woods
Is my elder brother, to a certainty!

Just as one who his own tomb sees,
Embitteredly it appears to me,
In the light of the American plenilune,
In the crepuscular soul of my race
As if a very vocation for Disgrace,
An ancestral tropism for Misfortune.

Then, foul, comes, rubbing plebeian
Sores, within the desert of ideas
Bearing the endemic despair of hell,
With a stark face, tattooed by smut,
This miner of the origins, the nut,
The Modern Philosopher, I'd tell!

---

[*] Metaphysicalness *n. neol.* The Portuguese noun *metafisicismo* means 'the domain or influence of metaphysics,' 'the subtlety, sophistication, complexity of metaphysics.'

Quis compreender, quebrando estéreis normas,
A vida fenomênica das Formas,
Que, iguais a fogos passageiros, luzem...
E apenas encontrou na idéia gasta
O horror dessa mecânica nefasta,
A que todas as coisas se reduzem!

E hão de achá-lo, amanhã, bestas agrestes,
Sobre a esteira sarcófaga das pestes
A mostrar, já nos últimos momentos,
Como quem se submete a uma charqueada,
Ao clarão tropical da luz danada,
O espólio dos seus dedos peçonhentos.

Tal a finalidade dos estames!
Mas ele viverá, rotos os liames
Dessa estranguladora lei que aperta
Todos os agregados perecíveis,
Nas eterizações indefiníveis
Da energia intra-atômica liberta!

Será calor, causa úbiqua de gozo,
Raio X, magnetismo misterioso,
Quimiotaxia, ondulação aérea,
Fonte de repulsões e de prazeres,
Sonoridade potencial dos seres,
Estrangulada dentro da matéria!

He wanted to, breaking sterile norms,
Grasp the phenomenic life of Forms,
Which, equal to passing fires, glow...
And only found in the idea outworn
Of that nefast mechanics the horror,
To which all things are reduced so!

Find him next, shall beasts agrestial,
On a sarcophagous wake, pestilential,
Already in his last moments showing,
As one submitted to a jerking[*] might,
In the tropical glare of a damned light,
From his poisonous fingers the spoiling.

Here the finality of stamina lies!
But he shall live, broken the ties
Of the strangling law which squeezes
All the perishable aggregations,
In the indefinable etherizations
Of intra-atomic energy released!

He'll be heat, joy's cause ubiquitous,
X-ray, magnetism mysterious,
Chemotaxy, undulation of air,
Source of repulse and pleasures,
Potential sonority of creatures,
Strangled inside the matter!

---

[*] Jerking *pres. part. v.* Jerk, 'to cut into long slices or strips and dry in the sun (as meat).'

E o que ele foi: clavículas, abdômen,
O coração, a boca, em síntese, o Homem,
— Engrenagem de vísceras vulgares —
Os dedos carregados de peçonha,
Tudo coube na lógica medonha
Dos apodrecimentos musculares!

A desarrumação dos intestinos
Assombra! Vede-a! Os vermes assassinos
Dentro daquela massa que o húmus come,
Numa glutoneria hedionda, brincam,
Como as cadelas que as dentuças trincam
No espasmo fisiológico da fome.

É uma trágica festa emocionante!
A bacteriologia inventariante
Toma conta do corpo que apodrece...
E até os membros da família engulham,
Vendo as larvas malignas que se embrulham
No cadáver malsão, fazendo um *s*.

E foi então para isto que esse doudo
Estragou o vibrátil plasma todo,
À guisa de um faquir, pelos cenóbios?!...
Num suicídio graduado, consumir-se,
E após tantas vigílias, reduzir-se
À herança miserável de micróbios!

And what he was: clavicles, abdomen,
Heart, mouth, in synthesis, Man,
— Vulgar viscera's gearing —
His fingers with poison filled,
All in the dreadful logic befitted
Of the muscular putrefying!

The disarrangement of intestines
Amazes! See it! Vermin assassins,
Within that mass by humus eaten,
Play, in so hideous a gluttony,
Like bitches crunching toothily
In physiologic spasms of famine.

It's a tragic feast, so touching!
Bacteriology, inventorying,
Takes over the corpse that rots…
Even family folk feel nauseous,
Seeing ensnarled larvae, noxious,
In the ill cadaver in an *s* contort.

Hence was it, then, that the nut
All vibratile plasma spoiled up,
In guise of a fakir, for coenobes?!…
In a graduated suicide consumed,
And after so many vigils, reduced
To a miserable heirship of microbes!

Estoutro agora é o sátiro peralta
Que o sensualismo sodomita exalta,
Nutrindo sua infâmia a leite e a trigo...
Como que, em suas células vilíssimas,
Há estratificações requintadíssimas
De uma animalidade sem castigo.

Brancas bacantes bêbadas o beijam.
Suas artérias híricicas latejam,
Sentindo o odor das carnações abstêmias,
E à noite, vai gozar, ébrio de vício,
No sombrio bazar do meretrício,
O cuspo afrodisíaco das fêmeas.

No horror de sua anômala nevrose,
Toda a sensualidade da simbiose,
Uivando, à noite, em lúbricos arroubos,
Como no babilônico *sansara*,
Lembra a fome incoercível que escancara
A mucosa carnívora dos lobos.

Sôfrego, o monstro as vítimas aguarda.
Negra paixão congênita, bastarda,
Do seu zooplasma ofídico resulta...
E explode, igual à luz que o ar acomete,
Com a veemência mavórtica do aríete
E os arremessos de uma catapulta.

Another is the prankish satyr, now,
Who exalts a sensualism sodomitical,
Nursing on milk and wheat his infamy...
It is as if, within his vilest cells,
There be stratifications most swell
Of an animality without penalty.

Drunken white bacchantes kiss
Him. Palpitate his hircine arteries,
The odor of abstemious flesh sensing;
At night he enjoys, inebriated viciously,
At the somber bazaar of harlotry,
Of females the aphrodisiac spitting.

In the horror of anomalous neurosis,
All the sensuality of the symbiosis,
Howling at night in raptures lubricous,
As in a Babylon's *sansara*,[*] reminds of
The incoercible hunger which shows off
The mucosa of wolves, carnivorous.

The monster victims awaits, ravenous.
Black congenital passion, bastardous,
From his ophidian zooplasm results...
And explodes, as light charges the airs,
With the martial vehemence of an aries[†]
And else the shootings of a catapult.

[*] Sansara *n.* Either the Babylonian ritual of sacred prostitution, or the so-called Babylonian 'marriage market.'
[†] Aries *n. neol.* Ram, *specif* battering ram.

Mas muitas vezes, quando a noite avança,
Hirto, observa através a tênue trança
Dos filamentos fluídicos de um halo
A destra descarnada de um duende,
Que, tateando nas tênebras, se estende
Dentro da noite má, para agarrá-lo!

Cresce-lhe a intracefálica tortura,
E de su'alma na caverna escura,
Fazendo ultra-epilépticos esforços,
Acorda, com os candieiros apagados,
Numa coreografia de danados,
A família alarmada dos remorsos.

É o despertar de um povo subterrâneo!
É a fauna cavernícola do crânio
— Macbeths da patológica vigília,
Mostrando, em rembrandtescas telas várias,
As incestuosidades sanguinárias
Que ele tem praticado na família.

As alucinações tácteis pululam.
Sente que megatérios o estrangulam...
A asa negra das moscas o horroriza;
E autopsiando a amaríssima existência
Encontra um cancro assíduo na consciência
E três manchas de sangue na camisa!

But often, stiff, when night runs late,
He observes, through the tenuous plait
Of the fluidic filaments of a halo,
A goblin's fleshless dextral hand,
Groping in tenebrosity, extend
Within the evil night, to grip him so!

Increases his intracephalic torture,
And from his soul in a cave obscure,
Striving by ultra-epileptic efforts,
Wakes, with the oil lamps spent,
In a choreography of the damned,
The alarmed family of remorses.

The waking of a folk subterraneous!
The cave-dwelling fauna of the cranium
— Macbeths of the pathologic vigily,[*]
In various Rembrandtesque canvases
Showing the sanguinary incestuousness
He has perpetrated in his family.

The tactile hallucinations pullulate.
He feels, by megatheria, strangulated...
Of black wings of flies he dismays;
Autopsying so bittersome an existence
Finds assiduous canker in his conscience
And on his shirt three bloodstains!

---

[*] Vigily *n. obs.* Vigil.

Míngua-se o combustível da lanterna
E a consciência do sátiro se inferna,
Reconhecendo, bêbedo de sono,
Na própria ânsia dionisíaca do gozo,
Essa necessidade de *horroroso*,
Que é talvez propriedade do carbono!

Ah! Dentro de toda a alma existe a prova
De que a dor como um dartro se renova,
Quando o prazer barbaramente a ataca...
Assim também, observa a ciência crua,
Dentro da elipse ignívoma da lua
A realidade de uma esfera opaca.

Somente a Arte, esculpindo a humana mágoa,
Abranda as rochas rígidas, torna água
Todo o fogo telúrico profundo
E reduz, sem que, entanto, a desintegre,
À condição de uma planície alegre
A aspereza orográfica do mundo!

Provo desta maneira ao mundo odiento
Pelas grandes razões do sentimento,
Sem os métodos da abstrusa ciência fria
E os trovões gritadores da dialética,
Que a mais alta expressão da dor estética
Consiste essencialmente na alegria.

Augusto dos Anjos - *I*

Lessens the combustible of the lantern;
The satyr's conscience itself torments,
Recognizing, drunk with somnolency,
In his own Dionysiac anxiety for delight,
This need of the *horrible*, which might
Well be, perhaps, carbon's property!

Ah! Inside every soul proof there is
That sorrow like a dartre reappears,
When pleasure attacks it barbarously...
Thus crude science observes, too,
In the ignivomous ellipse of the moon,
Of an opaque sphere the reality.

Only Art, sculpting human grief,
Softens the rigid rocks, all deep
Telluric fire into water converts,
Reduces, yet without disintegration,
To a cheerful prairie's condition
The orographic asperity of the earth!

So I prove to the odious world, then,
Through the grand reasons of sentiment,
Without methods of cold abstruse science
And the bawling thunders of dialectics,
That the highest expression of aesthetic
Pain consists of gladness, in essence.

Continua o martírio das criaturas:
— O homicídio nas vielas mais escuras,
— O ferido que a hostil gleba atra escarva,
— O último solilóquio dos suicidas —
E eu sinto a dor de todas essas vidas
Em minha vida anônima de larva!"

Disse isto a Sombra. E, ouvindo estes vocábulos,
Da luz da lua aos pálidos venábulos,
Na ânsia de um nervosíssimo entusiasmo,
Julgava ouvir monótonas corujas,
Executando, entre caveiras sujas,
A orquestra arrepiadora do sarcasmo!

Era a elégia panteísta do Universo,
Na podridão do sangue humano imerso,
Prostituído talvez, em suas bases...
Era a canção da Natureza exausta,
Chorando e rindo na ironia infausta
Da incoerência infernal daquelas frases.

E o turbilhão de tais fonemas acres
Trovejando grandíloquos massacres,
Há de ferir-me as auditivas portas,
Até que minha efêmera cabeça
Reverta à quietação da treva espessa
E à palidez das fotosferas mortas!

Continues the martyrdom of creatures:
— Homicide on alleys most obscure,
— The wounded the dark hostile glebe hides,
— The last soliloquy of the suicidal —
And I feel the pain of these lives all
Within my larva's anonymous life!"

Said so the Shadow. And as I did hear
Such words, in moonlight's pale spears,
Anxious of a most nervous enthusiasm,
Monotone owls I guess I was hearing,
In the midst of soiled skulls, executing
The terrifying orchestra of sarcasm!

It was a pantheistic elegy of the Universe,
In putrescence of human blood immersed,
Prostituted, perhaps, on its very bases...
It was the exhausted Nature's melody,
Crying and laughing with infaust irony
At the infernal incoherence of such phrases.

And such acrid phonemes' whirlwind
Grandiloquent massacres thundering,
My auditive doors shall then pierce,
Until this ephemeral head of mine
Revert to the quiet of the thick night
And the pallor of dead photospheres!

O Morcego

Meia-noite. Ao meu quarto me recolho.
Meu Deus! E este morcego! E, agora, vede:
Na bruta ardência orgânica da sede,
Morde-me a goela ígneo e escaldante molho.

"Vou mandar levantar outra parede..."
— Digo. Ergo-me a tremer. Fecho o ferrolho
E olho o teto. E vejo-o ainda, igual a um olho,
Circularmente sobre a minha rede!

Pego de um pau. Esforços faço. Chego
A tocá-lo. Minha alma se concentra.
Que ventre produziu tão feio parto?!

A Consciência Humana é este morcego!
Por mais que a gente faça, à noite, ele entra
Imperceptivelmente em nosso quarto!

The Bat

Midnight. To recoil in my chamber I walk.
My God! And this bat! Now look, just:
In the brute organic ardency of thirst,
Bites my gullet an igneous scalding stock.

"Have another wall built up, I must…"
— I say. I raise trembling, bolt the lock,
Look at the ceiling. Over my hammock
I see it still, like an eye, circle headfirst!

I take up a stick. Efforts I make. I get
Even to touch it. My soul concentrates.
What womb such ugly birth engenders?!

The Human Conscience is this very bat!
Despite all we do, at night, it penetrates
Imperceptibly into our own chamber!

Psicologia de um Vencido

Eu, filho do carbono e do amoníaco,
Monstro de escuridão e rutilância,
Sofro, desde a epigênesis da infância,
A influência má dos signos do zodíaco.

Profundissimamente hipocondríaco,
Este ambiente me causa repugnância...
Sobe-me à boca uma ânsia análoga à ânsia
Que se escapa da boca de um cardíaco.

Já o verme — este operário das ruínas —
Que o sangue podre das carnificinas
Come, e à vida em geral declara guerra,

Anda a espreitar meus olhos para roê-los,
E há de deixar-me apenas os cabelos,
Na frialdade inorgânica da terra!

Psychology of a Loser

I, son of carbon and of ammoniac,[*]
Monster of obscurity and rutilance,
Suffer, since the epigenesis of infance,[†]
The evil influence of the signs of zodiac.

Most profoundly hypochondriac,
This ambient arouses my repugnance...
Up my mouth comes an urge as urgence
Escaping from the mouth of a cardiac.

Now the worm — laborer of the ruins —,
The rotten blood of carnage devouring,
And declaring war to life all around,

Is spying my eyes so as to gnaw them,
And shall leave me only my hair, then,
In the inorganic coldness of the ground!

---

[*] Ammoniac *n. neol.* Ammonia.
[†] Infance *n. obs.* Infancy.

A Ideia

De onde ela vem? De que matéria bruta
Vem essa luz que sobre as nebulosas
Cai de incógnitas criptas misteriosas
Como as estalactites duma gruta?

Vem da psicogenética e alta luta
Do feixe de moléculas nervosas,
Que, em desintegrações maravilhosas,
Delibera, e depois, quer e executa!

Vem do encéfalo absconso que a constringe,
Chega em seguida às cordas da laringe,
Tísica, tênue, mínima, raquítica...

Quebra a força centrípeta que a amarra,
Mas, de repente, e quase morta, esbarra
No mulambo da língua paralítica!

The Idea

Whence does it come? From whatever
Crude matter comes this light falling sur[*]
Nebulae of unknown crypts, mysterious,
Like the stalactites inside a cavern?

Comes from the psychogenetic and stern
Battle of a fascicle of molecules nervous
Which, in disintegrations marvelous,
Deliberates, and then wants and exerts!

From the absconse[†] encephalon constringing it,
To arrive, after, at the cords of the larynx,
Phthisic, tenuous, minimal, rachitic…

Breaks the centripetal force to which it's tied,
But suddenly, and almost dead, it collides
With the tatter of a tongue paralytic!

---

[*] Sur *prep*. On, upon.
[†] Absconse *adj. neol*. Absconded, concealed.

Idealização da Humanidade Futura

Rugia nos meus centros cerebrais
A multidão dos séculos futuros
— Homens que a herança de ímpetos impuros
Tornara etnicamente irracionais! —

Não sei que livro, em letras garrafais,
Meus olhos liam! No húmus dos monturos,
Realizavam-se os partos mais obscuros,
Dentre as genealogias animais!

Como quem esmigalha protozoários
Meti todos os dedos mercenários
Na consciência daquela multidão...

E, em vez de achar a luz que os Céus inflama,
Somente achei moléculas de lama
E a mosca alegre da putrefação!

Idealization of Future Humanity

Roared a multitude, in my cerebral
Core, from centuries of the future
— Men which the heritage of impure
Impetuses made ethnically irrational! —

I know not the book, in huge letters all,
My eyes read! In the humus of manures,
Were realized births the most obscure,
Amongst the genealogies of animals!

Like one who protozoans crushes,
Every mercenary finger I thrusted
Into that multitude's conscience…

Instead of light which the Heavens burns,
I have solely found molecules of dirt
And the happy fly of putrescence!

As Cismas do Destino

I

Recife. Ponte Buarque de Macedo.
Eu, indo em direção à casa do Agra,
Assombrado com a minha sombra magra,
Pensava no Destino, e tinha medo!

Na austera abóbada alta o fósforo alvo
Das estrelas luzia... O calçamento
Sáxeo, de asfalto rijo, atro e vidrento,
Copiava a polidez de um crânio calvo.

Lembro-me bem. A ponte era comprida,
E a minha sombra enorme enchia a ponte,
Como uma pele de rinoceronte
Estendida por toda a minha vida!

A noite fecundava o ovo dos vícios
Animais. Do carvão da treva imensa
Caía um ar danado de doença
Sobre a cara geral dos edifícios!

Tal uma horda feroz de cães famintos,
Atravessando uma estação deserta,
Uivava dentro do *eu*, com a boca aberta,
A matilha espantada dos instintos!

The Misgivings of Destiny

I

Recife. Buarque de Macedo Bridge.
Going toward Agra's funeral home, I,
Haunted by this lean shadow of mine,
Thought of Destiny, with fear sieged!

The stars, in the austere high vault,
Shone phosphorous white... A petrous
Paving, of rigid asphalt, dark, vitreous,
Copied the polish of a cranium bald.

I remember well. The bridge was long,
My shadow filled the bridge, enormous,
Just like the hide of some rhinoceros
Extended over my entire life long!

Night fecundated the egg of beastly
Vices. From the coal of immense dark
A damned air of disease lowered stark
On the general face of the buildings!

As a feral horde of famished hounds,
Through a desert station crossing,
The aghast pack of instincts howling
Was inside my *self*, with open mouths!

Era como se, na alma da cidade,
Profundamente lúbrica e revolta,
Mostrando as carnes, uma besta solta
Soltasse o berro da animalidade.

E aprofundando o raciocínio obscuro,
Eu vi, então, à luz de áureos reflexos,
O trabalho genésico dos sexos,
Fazendo à noite os homens do Futuro.

Livres de microscópios e escalpelos,
Dançavam, parodiando saraus cínicos,
Bilhões de *centrossomas* apolíneos
Na câmara promíscua do *vitellus*.

Mas, a irritar-me os globos oculares,
Apregoando e alardeando a cor nojenta,
Fetos magros, ainda na placenta,
Estendiam-me as mãos rudimentares!

Mostravam-me o apriorismo incognoscível
Dessa fatalidade igualitária,
Que fez minha família originária
Do antro daquela fábrica terrível!

A corrente atmosférica mais forte
Zunia. E, na ígnea crosta do Cruzeiro,
Julgava eu ver o fúnebre candieiro
Que há de me alumiar na hora da morte.

It was as if, in the soul of the city,
Profoundly revolting and lewd,
Showing its flesh, a beast, loose,
Let out the bellow of animality.

Fathoming the ratiocination obscure,
I saw, in the light of aureate reflexes,
The genesic laboring of the sexes,
Making at night men of the Future.

From microscopes and scalpels free,
Parodying cynic soirées, danced some
Billions of apollonic *centrosomes*
In the *vitellus* chamber of promiscuity.

But, irritant to my ocular globes,
Heralding and flaunting lousy hues,
Still in the placenta, scrawny fetuses
Their rudimentary hands unfolded!

They the incognoscible apriorism
Showed me, of the equalitarian fatality
Which had made my family originary
From that terrible factory's antrum!

The atmospheric current in greater power
Whistled. And, on the Crux's[*] igneous
Crust, I thought I saw the funebrious
Lamp that'll enlight me in death's hour.

---

[*] The Southern Cross constellation.

Ninguém compreendia o meu soluço,
Nem mesmo Deus! Da roupa pelas brechas,
O vento bravo me atirava flechas
E aplicações hiemais de gelo russo.

A vingança dos mundos astronômicos
Enviava à terra extraordinária faca,
Posta em rija adesão de goma laca
Sobre os meus elementos anatômicos.

Ah! Com certeza, Deus me castigava!
Por toda a parte, como um réu confesso,
Havia um juiz que lia o meu processo
E uma forca especial que me esperava!

Mas o vento cessara por instantes
Ou, pelo menos, o *ignis sapiens* do Orco
Abafava-me o peito arqueado e porco
Num núcleo de substâncias abrasantes.

É bem possível que eu um dia cegue.
No ardor desta letal tórrida zona,
A cor do sangue é a cor que me impressiona
E a que mais neste mundo me persegue!

Nobody comprehended my sobbing,
Not even God! Through rents of cloth,
The fierce wind at me arrows shot
And applied hiemal Russian frosting.

The vengeance of astronomic worlds
To earth an extraordinary knife sent,
To take, with lac wax rigid adherence,
Of all my anatomic elements hold.

Ah! God was chastising me, for sure!
Everywhere, as a felon who confessed,
There was a judge reading my process,
A special gallows awaiting my capture.

But the wind had ceased a few instants
Or, at least, the Orcus's *ignis sapiens*[*]
Was stifling my chest, filthy and bent,
In some nucleus of blazing substances.

It's quite possible I'll be blind one day.
In the ardor of this lethal torrid zone,
Impresses me a blood tone that is a tone
Which most in the world makes me prey!

---

[*] Ignis sapiens *phr*. From Latin, *lit.* 'sapient fire,' then 'judicious fire, phrase coined by the first Christian apologists. Orcus, like the Greek Hades, is either a god of the underworld who judges the dead in the afterlife, or the underworld itself, in the Etruscan and Roman mythologies.

Essa obsessão cromática me abate.
Não sei por que me vêm sempre à lembrança
O estômago esfaqueado de uma criança
E um pedaço de víscera escarlate.

Quisera qualquer coisa provisória
Que a minha cerebral caverna entrasse,
E até ao fim, cortasse e recortasse
A faculdade aziaga da memória.

Na ascensão barométrica da calma,
Eu bem sabia, ansiado e contrafeito,
Que uma população doente do peito
Tossia sem remédio na minh'alma!

E o cuspo que essa hereditária tosse
Golfava, à guisa de ácido resíduo,
Não era o cuspo só de um indivíduo
Minado pela tísica precoce.

Não! Não era o meu cuspo, com certeza
Era a expectoração pútrida e crassa
Dos brônquios pulmonares de uma raça
Que violou as leis da Natureza!

Era antes uma tosse úbiqua, estranha,
Igual ao ruído de um calhau redondo
Arremessado, no apogeu do estrondo,
Pelos fundibulários da montanha!

Augusto dos Anjos - *I*

This chromatic obsession ails me, thus.
I know not why it always comes to mind
A child's stomach stabbed with a knife
And some piece of its scarlet viscus.

How I wish anything provisory
My cerebral cavern would enter,
And cut and recut, until the end,
The inauspicious faculty of memory.

In a barometric ascension of calmness,
I knew well, gasping and disfigured,
That a population with a lung seizure
Coughed within my soul, remediless!

And the spit this hereditary tussis
Gushed, in the guise of acid residual,
Wasn't the spit of one only individual
Undermined by a precocious phthisis.

No! It was not my spit, for it sure
Was the expectoration, putrid, dense,
From the pulmonary bronchi of a race
Which violated the laws of Nature!

Rather a ubiquitous tussis, strange,
Equal to the noise of a rounded stone,
In the apogee of the rumble, thrown
By slingshooters of a mountain range!

E a saliva daqueles infelizes
Inchava, em minha boca, de tal arte,
Que eu, para não cuspir por toda a parte,
Ia engolindo, aos poucos, a hemoptísis!

Na alta alucinação de minhas cismas,
O microcosmos líquido da gota
Tinha a abundância de uma artéria rota,
Arrebentada pelos aneurismas.

Chegou-me o estado máximo da mágoa!
Duas, três, quatro, cinco, seis e sete
Vezes que eu me furei com um canivete,
A hemoglobina vinha cheia de água!

Cuspo, cujas caudais meus beiços regam,
Sob a forma de mínimas camândulas,
Benditas sejam todas essas glândulas,
Que, quotidianamente, te segregam!

Escarrar de um abismo noutro abismo,
Mandando ao Céu o fumo de um cigarro,
Há mais filosofia neste escarro
Do que em toda a moral do Cristianismo!

Porque, se no orbe oval que os meus pés tocam
Eu não deixasse o meu cuspo carrasco,
Jamais exprimiria o acérrimo asco
Que os canalhas do mundo me provocam!

And the saliva of all of the miserable
Bloated, in my mouth, in such a way,
That I, not to spit in every which way,
Gulped the hemoptysis, little by little!

Highly hallucinated by my misgivings,
The microcosmos of a drop, watery,
Had the abundance of a spoiled artery,
All bursting up with aneurysms.

My grief arrived at a maximum state!
Two, three, four, five, six, seven times
I pricked myself with a switch knife,
The hemoglobin came water-saturate!

Spit, whose torrents my lips bedew,
In the shape of minute beads,
All those glandulae, blessed be,
Which, quotidianly, secrete you!

To sputter from abysm to other abysm,
Sending fume of a cigarette to Heaven,
More philosophy in this sputter is than
In the entire moral of Christianism!

For, if on the oval orb my feet touch
Had I not left my scabrous sputter,
I'd never, my acridest disgust, utter,
Provoked in me by the villains on earth!

II

Foi no horror dessa noite tão funérea
Que eu descobri, maior talvez que Vinci,
Com a força visualística do lince,
A falta de unidade na matéria!

Os esqueletos desarticulados,
Livres do acre fedor das carnes mortas,
Rodopiavam, com as brancas tíbias tortas,
Numa dança de números quebrados!

Todas as divindades malfazejas,
Siva e Arimã, os duendes, o In e os trasgos,
Imitando o barulho dos engasgos,
Davam pancadas no adro das igrejas.

Nessa hora de monólogos sublimes,
A companhia dos ladrões da noite,
Buscando uma taverna que os acoite,
Vai pela escuridão pensando crimes.

Perpetravam-se os atos mais funestos,
E o luar, da cor de um doente de icterícia,
Iluminava, a rir, sem pudicícia,
A camisa vermelha dos incestos.

II

In the horror of this night so funereal
I discovered, greater perhaps than Vinci,
With the visualistic[*] force of the lynx,
The lack of unity in what is material!

The disarticulated skeletons, freed
From the dead flesh's acrid stench,
Spun round, with white tibiae bent,
In some dance of broken figures!

Every one of the divinities maleficent,
Shiva, Ahriman, elfs, the Yin, goblins,
Imitating from gaggings the noising,
Gave on the atrium of churches a bang.

At this hour of monologues sublime,
The night thieves, in a band gathered,
Seeking a tavern to give them shelter,
Go through darkness thinking crimes.

Perpetrated were the most funest acts,
The moon, the color of one ill of jaundice,
Illumined, laughing, without pudicity,
The vermillion chemise of incests.

---

[*] Visualistic *adj. neol.* Visual (in the original, *visualística* is also a neologism by dos Anjos).

Ninguém, de certo, estava ali, a espiar-me,
Mas um lampião, lembrava ante o meu rosto,
Um sugestionador olho, ali posto
De propósito, para hipnotizar-me!

Em tudo, então, meus olhos distinguiram,
Da miniatura singular de uma aspa
À anatomia mínima da caspa,
Embriões de mundos que não progrediram!

Pois quem não vê aí, em qualquer rua,
Com a fina nitidez de um claro jorro,
Na paciência budista do cachorro
A alma embrionária que não continua?!

Ser cachorro! Ganir incompreendidos
Verbos! Querer dizer-nos que não finge,
E a palavra embrulhar-se no laringe,
Escapando-se apenas em latidos!

Despir a putrescível forma tosca,
Na atra dissolução que tudo inverte,
Deixar cair sobre a barriga inerte
O apetite necrófago da mosca!

A alma dos animais! Pego-a, distingo-a,
Acho-a nesse interior duelo secreto
Entre a ânsia de um vocábulo completo
E uma expressão que não chegou à língua!

Augusto dos Anjos - *I*

No one, for certain, was there to spy me,
But a lamppost recalled, 'fore my face,
A suggestioning eye, there just placed
On purpose, so as to hypnotize me!

In all my eyes distinguished, so,
From a quote's singular miniature
To the anatomy of a scurf, minute,
Unprogressed worlds' embryos!

For whoever sees not then, on any street,
With fine neatness of a clear gush forth,
In the dog's Buddhist patient sloth
The embrionary soul which doesn't keep?!

To be a dog! To yowl misunderstanding
Verbs! To want to tell us it feigns not,
And the word in its larynx itself knots,
Merely escaping it with its barking!

To bare the putrescible coarse form by
The noxious dissolution that all inverts,
To let drown upon its own belly, inert,
The necrophagous appetite of the fly!

The soul of animals! I take, distinguish,
Find it in this interior duel, secret,
Between anxiety of a vocable complete
And expression into tongue unfinished!

Surpreendo-a em quatrilhões de corpos vivos,
Nos antiperistálticos abalos
Que produzem nos bois e nos cavalos
A contração dos gritos instintivos!

Tempo viria, em que, daquele horrendo
Caos de corpos orgânicos disformes
Rebentariam cérebros enormes,
Como bolhas febris de água, fervendo!

Nessa época que os sábios não ensinam,
A pedra dura, os montes argilosos
Criariam feixes de cordões nervosos
E o neuroplasma dos que raciocinam!

Almas pigmeias! Deus subjuga-as, cinge-as
À imperfeição! Mas vem o Tempo, e vence-O,
E o meu sonho crescia no silêncio,
Maior que as epopeias carolíngias!

Era a revolta trágica dos tipos
Ontogênicos mais elementares,
Desde os foraminíferos dos mares
À grei liliputiana dos polipos.

Todos os personagens da tragédia,
Cansados de viver na paz de Buda,
Pareciam pedir com a boca muda
A ganglionária célula intermédia.

Augusto dos Anjos - *I*

In quadrillion living bodies I surprise it,
In the antiperistaltic shocks
Producing in horses and bullocks
The contractions of the cries of instinct!

Time would come when, from abhorrent
Chaos of deformed organic bodies out,
Enormous cerebrums would sprout,
Like feverish water bubbles, fervent!

In such epoch that the sages don't lesson,
The hard rock, the argillous peaks
Would create nervous cords' sheaves
And the neuroplasm of those who reason!

Pygmy souls! God subjugates, binds them
To imperfection! But comes Time, and Him
Defeats, and in silence increased my dream,
Greater than the epopees of the Carolingian!

It was the tragic revolt of the most
Elementary ontogenic species,
From the foraminifera of the seas
To the polyps' lilliputian host.

All the personages of this tragedy,
Fatigued of living in Buddha's peace,
Seemed with mute mouth to plead
The ganglionary cell as intermediary.

A planta que a canícula ígnea torra,
E as coisas inorgânicas mais nulas
Apregoavam encéfalos, medulas
Na alegria guerreira da desforra!

Os protistas e o obscuro acervo rijo
Dos espongiários e dos infusórios
Recebiam com os seus órgãos sensórios
O triunfo emocional do regozijo.

E apesar de já ser assim tão tarde,
Aquela humanidade parasita,
Como um bicho inferior, berrava, aflita,
No meu temperamento de covarde!

Mas, refletindo, a sós, sobre o meu caso,
Vi que, igual a um amniota subterrâneo,
Jazia atravessada no meu crânio
A intercessão fatídica do atraso!

A hipótese genial do *microzima*
Me estrangulava o pensamento guapo,
E eu me encolhia todo como um sapo
Que tem um peso incômodo por cima!

Nas agonias do *delirium-tremens*,
Os bêbedos alvares que me olhavam,
Com os copos cheios esterilizavam
A substância prolífica dos sêmens!

Augusto dos Anjos - I

The plant the igneous canicule burns,
And the most null inorganic things,
Encephala, medullae were heralding,
With the redress's warriorlike fun!

The protists and the rigid lot, obscure,
Of the spongiae and the infusorians
Received with their sensory organs
The emotional triumph of pleasure!

And though it already did so laten,
That parasite humanity, afflicted,
Like an inferior beast screeched
In my temperament of a craven!

But reflecting, all alone, on my condition
I saw, as an amniote subterraneous,
It was laid crosswise in my cranium
The backwardness's fateful intercession!

The *microzime*'s hypothesis of genius
My doughty thought so strangled,
And I shrank entirely like a toad
O'er which is a weight incommodious!

In the agonies of a *delirium tremens*,
Looking at me, the drunkards, fool,
Sterilized, with their glasses full,
The prolific substance of semens!

Enterravam as mãos dentro das goelas,
E sacudidos de um tremor indômito
Expeliam, na dor forte do vômito,
Um conjunto de gosmas amarelas.

Iam depois dormir nos lupanares
Onde, na glória da concupiscência,
Depositavam quase sem consciência
As derradeiras forças musculares.

Fabricavam destarte os blastodermas,
Em cujo repugnante receptáculo
Minha perscrutação via o espetáculo
De uma progênie idiota de palermas.

Prostituição ou outro qualquer nome,
Por tua causa, embora o homem te aceite,
É que as mulheres ruins ficam sem leite
E os meninos sem pai morrem de fome!

Por que há de haver aqui tantos enterros?
Lá no "Engenho" também, a morte é ingrata...
Há o malvado carbúnculo que mata
A sociedade infante dos bezerros!

Burying hands down their gullets to,
With indomitable tremor shaking,
Expel, in a vomit strong aching,
A whole mass of yellowish goo.

Then, in lupanars to sleep they went,
Where, in the glory of concupiscence,
They deposed almost without conscience
Their hindmost muscular strength.

They fabricated blastoderms, thus,
In whose repugnant receptacle
My perscrutation saw the spectacle
Of an idiotic progeny of dunces.

Prostitution or whatever you name it,
Because of you, though man acquiesces,
The wicked women remain milkless
And the fatherless boys die of famine!

Why shall so many burials here be?
Death is ingrate, also in the "Mill"...[*]
The malevolent carbuncle[†] there kills
Of the calves their infant society!

---

[*] The Mill of Pau d'Arco, a sugarcane mill, property of the poet's family, where he was born and raised (see Chronology).
[†] In Portuguese, the word can also refer to anthrax.

Quantas moças que o túmulo reclama!
E após a podridão de tantas moças,
Os porcos espojando-se nas poças
Da virgindade reduzida à lama!

Morte, ponto final da última cena,
Forma difusa da matéria imbele,
Minha filosofia te repele,
Meu raciocínio enorme te condena!

Diante de ti, nas catedrais mais ricas,
Rolam sem eficácia os amuletos,
Oh! Senhora dos nossos esqueletos
E das caveiras diárias que fabricas!

E eu desejava ter, numa ânsia rara,
Ao pensar nas pessoas que perdera,
A inconsciência das máscaras de cera
Que a gente prega, com um cordão, na cara!

Era um sonho ladrão de submergir-me
Na vida universal, e, em tudo imerso,
Fazer da parte abstrata do Universo,
Minha morada equilibrada e firme!

Nisto, pior que o remorso do assassino,
Reboou, tal qual, num fundo de caverna,
Numa impressionadora voz interna,
O eco particular do meu Destino:

How many girls the tomb requires!
And after putridity of so many girls,
The pigs wallowing in the puddles
Of virginity reduced to the mire!

Death, full point of the ultimate scene,
Diffuse form of matter imbellious,
My philosophy does so repel you,
Condemns you my enormous reasoning!

'Fore you, in the richest cathedrals,
Cooed are fecklessly the amulets,
Oh! Mistress of our skelets
And your fabricated daily skulls!

And I wish I had, in rare yearning,
When thinking of persons I lack,
The unconsciousness of wax masks
We fasten to our face with a string!

It was some thievish dream to souse
Into universal life and, in all immersed,
Make the abstract part of the Universe
My dwelling equilibrated and stout!

So, worse than remorse of an assassin,
Rumbled, as in the depth of a cavern,
In such an impressive voice, intern,[*]
The particular echo of my Destiny:

---

[*] Intern *adj. archaic.* Internal.

III

"Homem! por mais que a Idéia desintegres,
Nessas perquisições que não têm pausa,
Jamais, magro homem, saberás a causa
De todos os fenômenos alegres!

Em vão, com a bronca enxada árdega, sondas
A estéril terra, e a hialina lâmpada oca,
Trazes, por perscrutar (oh! ciência louca!)
O conteúdo das lágrimas hediondas.

Negro e sem fim é esse em que te mergulhas
Lugar do Cosmos, onde a dor infrene
É feita como é feito o querosene
Nos recôncavos úmidos das hulhas!

Porque, para que a Dor perscrutes, fora
Mister que, não como és, em síntese, antes
Fosses, a refletir teus semelhantes,
A própria humanidade sofredora!

A universal complexidade é que Ela
Compreende. E se, por vezes, se divide,
Mesmo ainda assim, seu todo não reside
No quociente isolado da parcela!

III

"Man! however disintegrate you might
The Idea, in perquisitions without pause,
Never, meager man, will you know the cause
Of every one phenomenon of delight!

In vain you sound, the rustic hoe toiling,
The sterile earth, and the hollow translucent
Lamp bring, to scrutinize (oh! mad science!)
The content of the gruesome weeping.

That's the Cosmos spot, black, endless,
You plunge in, where unbridled ache
Is made as kerosene likewise is made
Inside the peat coal's humid recesses!

Because, to scrutinize Sorrow, it'd be
Imperative, not as you are, in short,
You rather, to reflect a kindred sort,
Be the selfsame suffering humanity!

What It comprehends, is the universal
Complexity. And if sometimes it divides
Itself, nevertheless its whole resides
Not in the isolated quotient of a parcel!

Ah! Como o ar imortal a dor não finda!
Das papilas nervosas que há nos tatos
Veio e vai desde os tempos mais transatos
Para outros tempos que hão de vir ainda!

Como o machucamento das insônias
Te estraga, quando toda a estuada Idéia
Dás ao sôfrego estudo da ninféia
E de outras plantas dicotiledôneas!

A diáfana água alvíssima e a hórrida áscua
Que da ígnea flama bruta, estriada, espirra;
A formação molecular da mirra,
O cordeiro simbólico da Páscoa;

As rebeladas cóleras que rugem
No homem civilizado, e a ele se prendem
Como às pulseiras que os mascates vendem
A aderência teimosa da ferrugem;

O orbe feraz que bastos tojos acres
Produz; a rebelião que, na batalha,
Deixa os homens deitados, sem mortalha,
Na sangueira concreta dos massacres;

Os sanguinolentíssimos chicotes
Da hemorragia; as nódoas mais espessas,
O achatamento ignóbil das cabeças,
Que ainda degrada os povos hotentotes;

Ah! As immortal air, ends not Sorrow!
From the nervous papillae of the tact
It came and goes since times far back
To other times that are yet to follow!

How it does spoil you so, the sore
Of insomnias, when every seethed Idea
You give to restless study of the nymphaea
And other dicotyledonous plants more!

Clearest diaphanous water, spark horrid
That from brute igneous flame, striate, stirs;
The molecular formation of the myrrh,
The Paschal Lamb of God, symbolic;

The rebelled cholers that burst
In civilized man, and in him entangle,
As, by peddlers vended, the bangles
To which adheres the stubborn rust;

The feracious orb that thick acrid whins
Yields; a rebellion that, in battle, there
Forsakes men laid down, shroud-bare,
In the massacres' concrete slaughtering;

The whiplashes most sanguinolent
Of hemorrhage; the grossest spots,
The ignoble flattening of head tops,
Still to the Hottentots' degradement;

O Amor e a Fome, a fera ultriz que o fojo
Entra, à espera que a mansa vítima o entre,
— Tudo que gera no materno ventre
A causa fisiológica do nojo;

As pálpebras inchadas na vigília,
As aves moças que perderam a asa,
O fogão apagado de uma casa,
Onde morreu o chefe da família;

O trem particular que um corpo arrasta
Sinistramente pela via férrea,
A cristalização da massa térrea,
O tecido da roupa que se gasta;

A água arbitrária que hiulcos caules grossos
Carrega e come; as negras formas feias
Dos aracnídeos e das centopeias,
O fogo-fátuo que ilumina os ossos;

As projeções flamívomas que ofuscam,
Como uma pincelada rembrandtesca,
A sensação que uma coalhada fresca
Transmite às mãos nervosas dos que a buscam;

O antagonismo de Tifon e Osíris,
O homem grande oprimindo o homem pequeno,
A lua falsa de um parasseleno,
A mentira meteórica do arco-íris;

Love and Famine, a beast in ultion[*] lust,
Awaiting the tame victim to the pitfall
Enter too — All that breeds in maternal
Womb the physiological cause of disgust;

The palpebrae swollen in vigil hours,
The young birds whose wing is gone,
The extinguished stove of a home
Whose head of the family passed out;

The particular train that has drawn,
Sinisterly, a corpse along the railway,
The crystallization of terrene mass lay,
The fabric of clothes outworn;

Arbitrary water carrying, eating hiatus
Thick stems; the ugly and obscure
Arachnida and centipede figures,
The bone-illuminating ignis fatuus;

Flame-vomit projections that obfuscate,
Like a Rembrandtesque brushstroke,
The sensation fresh clabber provokes
In the nervous hands of whom it takes;

Typhon and Osiris's antagonism,
The lofty man oppressing the mean
Man, the false moon of a paraselene,
The rainbow's meteoric untruism;

---

[*] Ultion *n. obs.* Revenge, vengeance, retaliation.

Os terremotos que, abalando os solos,
Lembram paióis de pólvora explodindo,
A rotação dos fluidos produzindo
A depressão geológica dos polos;

O instinto de procriar, a ânsia legítima
Da alma, afrontando ovante aziagos riscos,
O juramento dos guerreiros priscos
Metendo as mãos nas glândulas da vítima;

As diferenciações que o psicoplasma
Humano sofre na mania mística,
A pesada opressão característica
Dos 10 minutos de um acesso de asma;

E, (conquanto contra isto ódios regougues)
A utilidade fúnebre da corda
Que arrasta a rês, depois que a rês engorda,
À morte desgraçada dos açougues...

Tudo isto que o terráqueo abismo encerra
Forma a complicação desse barulho
Travado entre o dragão do humano orgulho
E as forças inorgânicas da terra!

Por descobrir tudo isso, embalde cansas!
Ignoto é o gérmen dessa força ativa
Que engendra, em cada célula passiva,
A heterogeneidade das mudanças!

Augusto dos Anjos - I

Earthquakes that the grounds tremble
Recall powder magazines exploding,
The rotation of the fluids molding
The geological depression of the poles;

The procreating instinct, legitime[*] angst
Of the soul, affronting, ovationed, risks
Ominous, priscan[†] warriors' oath, who stick
Their hands into their victim's glands;

Differentiations the human psychoplasm
Suffers with the mania of mystique,
The heavy oppression characteristic
Of a 10-minute access of asthma;

And, (though hate against it you mutter)
The funebrious utility of the rope that
Draws a beef, as the beef grows fat,
To its deplorable death at the butchers'...

All that the terraqueous abysm bounds
Forms the complicated brawl betwixt,
Engaged, the dragon of human conceit
And the inorganic forces of the ground.

To discover it all, vain is your wearying!
Ignote is the very germ of this active
Force which engenders, in each passive
Cell, the heterogeneity of the shiftings!

---

[*] Legitime *n. obs.* Legitimate.
[†] Priscan *adj. rare.* Ancient, old.

Poeta, feto malsão, criado com os sucos
De um leite mau, carnívoro asqueroso,
Gerado no atavismo monstruoso
Da alma desordenada dos malucos;

Última das criaturas inferiores
Governada por átomos mesquinhos,
Teu pé mata a uberdade dos caminhos
E esteriliza os ventres geradores!

O áspero mal que a tudo, em torno, trazes,
Análogo é ao que, negro e a seu turno,
Traz o ávido filóstomo noturno
Ao sangue dos mamíferos vorazes!

Ah! Por mais que, com o espírito, trabalhes
A perfeição dos seres existentes,
Hás de mostrar a cárie dos teus dentes
Na anatomia horrenda dos detalhes!

O Espaço — esta abstração spenceriana
Que abrange as relações de coexistência
É só! Não tem nenhuma dependência
Com as vértebras mortais da espécie humana!

As radiantes elipses que as estrelas
Traçam, e ao espectador falsas se antolham
São verdades de luz que os homens olham
Sem poder, no entretanto, compreendê-las.

Augusto dos Anjos - I

Poet, sickly fetus, nursed with juices
Of a bad milk, loathsomely carnivorous,
Generated in the atavism so monstrous
Of the disordered soul of the lunies;

The last of the inferior creatures
Governed by atoms thus measly,
Your foot kills the path's fecundity,
Sterilizes the generative uterus!

The harsh evil you bring around all,
Analogous is to what, black and in turn,
Brings the avid phyllostome, nocturn,[*]
To the blood of voracious mammals!

However much, with the spirit, travail
You the perfection of beings that exist,
The caries of your teeth you shall exhibit
With the horrendous anatomy of details!

This Spencerian abstraction — Space
— Encompassing relations of coexistence
Is sole! It has not any dependence
On mortal vertebrae of the human race!

The radiant ellipses which the stars
Trace, and to the spectator false appear
Are truths of light at which men peer
Though cannot understand so far.

---

[*] Nocturn *adj. archaic.* Nocturnal.

Em vão, com a mão corrupta, outro éter pedes,
Que essa mão, de esqueléticas falanges,
Dentro dessa água que com a vista abranges,
Também prova o princípio de Arquimedes!

A fadiga feroz que te esbordoa
Há de deixar-te essa medonha marca,
Que, nos corpos inchados de anasarca,
Deixam os dedos de qualquer pessoa!

Nem terás no trabalho que tiveste
A misericordiosa toalha amiga,
Que afaga os homens doentes de bexiga
E enxuga, à noite, as pústulas da peste!

Quando chegar depois a hora tranquila,
Tu serás arrastado, na carreira,
Como um cepo inconsciente de madeira
Na evolução orgânica da argila!

Um dia comparado com um milênio
Seja, pois, o teu último Evangelho...
É a evolução do novo para o velho
E do homogêneo para o heterogêneo!

Adeus! Fica-te aí, com o abdômen largo
A apodrecer!... És poeira, e embalde vibras!
O corvo que comer as tuas fibras
Há de achar nelas um sabor amargo!"

Augusto dos Anjos - *I*

In vain, with corrupt hand, other ether plead
You, for this skeletally phalangeal hand,
Inside water you with the view comprehend,
Also proves the principle of Archimedes!

The ferocious fatigue which beats
You, shall leave this dreadful mark
That, in bodies swollen by anasarca,
Any other person's fingers leave!

Nor have the merciful friendly towel,
In the toil you've had, you will,
That caresses men with smallpox ill,
Dries at night pustules pestilential!

When after comes the hour tranquil,
You will be dragged, in the current,
Like a stump of wood, unconscient,
In the organic evolution of the argil!

One day compared to a millennium,
Therefore, your last Evangel be so...
It's the evolution from new to old
And homogeneous to heterogeneous!

Farewell! Stay there, with a decaying
Fat abdomen!... You're dust, and thrill
In vain! The crow your fibers eats will
Find in them a rather bitter tasting!"

IV

Calou-se a voz. A noite era funesta.
E os queixos, a exibir trismos danados,
Eu puxava os cabelos desgrenhados
Como o Rei Lear, no meio da floresta!

Maldizia, com apóstrofes veementes,
No estentor de mil línguas insurretas,
O convencionalismo das Pandetas
E os textos maus dos códigos recentes!

Minha imaginação atormentada
Paria absurdos... Como diabos juntos,
Perseguiam-me os olhos dos defuntos
Com a carne da esclerótica esverdeada.

Secara a clorofila das lavouras.
Igual aos sustenidos de uma endecha,
Vinha-me às cordas glóticas a queixa
Das coletividades sofredoras.

O mundo resignava-se invertido
Nas forças principais do seu trabalho...
A gravidade era um princípio falho,
A análise espectral tinha mentido!

IV

Hushed the voice. The night was funest.
My jaws damned trismuses did display,
And I was pulling my hair in disarray
As King Lear, in the midst of the forest!

With vehement invectives I did maledict,
As a stentor of a thousand insurrected
Tongues, the conventions of Pandects
And of recent codes their bad scripts!

My tormented imagination delivered
Absurdities... Like devils together,
Persecuted me the eyes of cadavers
With the coat of their sclera greened.

Dried the chlorophyll of husbandries.
As the sharps of an endecha, came
To my glottic cords the complains
From the suffering collectivities.

The world itself was resigned,
Invert in its main forces of labor...
Gravity's principle was a failure,
The spectral analysis had lied!

O Estado, a Associação, os Municípios
Eram mortos. De todo aquele mundo
Restava um mecanismo moribundo
E uma teleologia sem princípios.

Eu queria correr, ir para o inferno,
Para que, da psiquê no oculto jogo,
Morressem sufocadas pelo fogo
Todas as impressões do mundo externo!

Mas a Terra negava-me o equilíbrio…
Na Natureza, uma mulher de luto
Cantava, espiando as árvores sem fruto,
A canção prostituta do ludíbrio.

State, Association, Municipality
Were dead. Of all that world but
Remained a mechanism moribund
And, lacking principles, a teleology.

I wanted to run, to go down to hell,
So that, in the psyche's occult game,
All died, suffocated by the flames,
The impressions of the world external!

But Earth denied me equilibrium...
In Nature, a woman in mourning
Sang, the fruitless trees observing,
The prostitute song of ludibrium![*]

---

[*] Ludibrium *n. archaic.* Derision, scorn.

Solitário

Como um fantasma que se refugia
Na solidão da natureza morta,
Por trás dos ermos túmulos, um dia,
Eu fui refugiar-me à tua porta!

Fazia frio e o frio que fazia
Não era esse que a carne nos conforta...
Cortava assim como em carniçaria
O aço das facas incisivas corta!

Mas tu não vieste ver minha Desgraça!
E eu saí, como quem tudo repele,
— Velho caixão a carregar destroços —

Levando apenas na tumbal carcaça
O pergaminho singular da pele
E o chocalho fatídico dos ossos!

Solitary

Like a ghost which takes shelter
In dead nature's solitude, laid
Behind the deserted sepulchers,
By your door I sheltered one day!

It was cold and the cold was never
Like one by flesh comfortable made...
It cut as, in the butchery, rather
Cuts the steel of incisive blades!

Yet, my Disgrace you came not to look on!
And I left, as one repelling everything,
— Old coffin wreckage bearing full —

Taking only, then, on my tombal carrion
The singular parchment of the skin
And of the bones the rattle fateful!

Idealismo

Falas de amor, e eu ouço tudo e calo!
O amor na Humanidade é uma mentira.
É. E é por isto que na minha lira
De amores fúteis poucas vezes falo.

O amor! Quando virei por fim a amá-lo?!
Quando, se o amor que a Humanidade inspira
É o amor do sibarita e da hetaíra,
De Messalina e de Sardanapalo?!

Pois é mister que, para o amor sagrado,
O mundo fique imaterializado
— Alavanca desviada do seu fulcro —

E haja só amizade verdadeira
Duma caveira para outra caveira,
Do meu sepulcro para o seu sepulcro?!

Idealism

You speak of love, I hear it all and hush!
Love within Humanity is some lie.
It is. And that's why, with my lyre,
Of futile love I scarcely speak much.

Love! When will I finally love it as such?!
When, if the love Humanity inspires
Is the love of hetaerae and sybarites,
Is Messalina's and Sardanapalus's lust?!

For is it imperious that, to a sacralized
Love, the world remain immaterialized
— A lever dislocated from its fulcrum —

And there be just friendship truthful
From the one skull to the other skull,
From my sepulchrum to your sepulchrum?!

Último Credo

Como ama o homem adúltero o adultério
E o ébrio a garrafa tóxica de rum,
Amo o coveiro — este ladrão comum
Que arrasta a gente para o cemitério!

É o transcendentalíssimo mistério!
É o *nous*, é o *pneuma*, é o *ego sum qui sum*,
É a morte, é esse danado número *Um*
Que matou Cristo e que matou Tibério!

Creio, como o filósofo mais crente,
Na generalidade decrescente
Com que a substância cósmica evolui...

Creio, perante a evolução imensa,
Que o homem universal de amanhã vença
O homem particular que eu ontem fui!

Last Creed

As loves adultery the man adulterous
And the inebriate a toxic bottle of rum,
I love the gravedigger — this common
Thief, who to a cemetery drags us!

It's most transcendentally mysterious!
Nous[*], *pneuma*[†], *ego sum qui sum*...[‡] In sum,
It's death, it's that damned number *One*
Which killed Christ and killed Tiberius!

I creed,[§] as philosopher most creeding,
In the generality insofar decreasing
With which evolves the cosmic substance...

I creed that, before evolution so vast,
The morrow universal man shall cast
Down the particular man I've been once!

---

[*] Nous *n*. From the Greek νους, mind, reason.
[†] Pneuma *n*. From the Greek πνευμα, wind, air, breath, spirit.
[‡] Ego sum qui sum *phr*. Latin for *I am that I am* (Exodus III, 14).
[§] Creed *vb. obs.* Believe.

Solilóquio de um Visionário

Para desvirginar o labirinto
Do velho e metafísico Mistério,
Comi meus olhos crus no cemitério,
Numa antropofagia de faminto!

A digestão desse manjar funéreo
Tornado sangue transformou-me o instinto
De humanas impressões visuais que eu sinto,
Nas divinas visões de íncola etéreo!

Vestido de hidrogênio incandescente,
Vaguei um século, improficuamente,
Pelas monotonias siderais...

Subi talvez às máximas alturas,
Mas, se hoje volto assim, com a alma às escuras,
É necessário que ainda eu suba mais!

Soliloquy of a Visionary

So as to deflower the labyrinth
Of the old and metaphysical Mystery,
I ate my crude[*] eyes at the cemetery,
An anthropophagus famished in't!

The digestion of this funereal savory,
Made blood, transformed my instinct,
From my sensed human visual imprint
To divine visions of ethereal tenantry!

By incandescent hydrogen covered,
A century, unprofitably, as a rover,
Through sidereal monotonies I did go...

To maximum heights I may have climbed,
But if now I'm back, my soul thus blinded,
It's necessary that I climb yet more so!

---

[*] Crude *adj. obs*. Raw.

Vozes da Morte

Agora, sim! Vamos morrer, reunidos,
Tamarindo da minha desventura,
Tu, com o envelhecimento da nervura,
Eu, com o envelhecimento dos tecidos!

Ah! Esta noite é a noite dos Vencidos!
E a podridão, meu velho! E essa futura
Ultrafatalidade de ossatura,
A que nos acharemos reduzidos!

Não morrerão, porém, tuas sementes!
E assim, para o Futuro, em diferentes
Florestas, vales, selvas, glebas, trilhos,

Na multiplicidade dos teus ramos,
Pelo muito que em vida nos amamos,
Depois da morte, inda teremos filhos!

Voices of Death

At last! Now we shall die, united,
Tamarind of my misadventure,
You, with the aging of the nervure,
I, with the tissues aging tight!

Ah! This night is the Losers' night!
And putridness, old chap! A future
Ultrafatality of carcass we'll sure
Find us reduced to in our plight!

Your seeds, though, won't die then!
Thus, for the Future, in different
Forests, valleys, jungles, glebes, paths,

In the multiplicity of your limbs,
For much in life one another loving,
We'll still have children after death!

O Martírio do Artista

Arte ingrata! E conquanto, em desalento,
A órbita elipsoidal dos olhos lhe arda,
Busca exteriorizar o pensamento
Que em suas fronetais células guarda!

Tarda-lhe a Ideia! A Inspiração lhe tarda!
E ei-lo a tremer, rasga o papel, violento,
Como o soldado que rasgou a farda
No desespero do último momento!

Tenta chorar e os olhos sente enxutos!...
É como o paralítico que, à míngua
Da própria voz e na que ardente o lavra

Febre de em vão falar, com os dedos brutos
Para falar, puxa e repuxa a língua,
E não lhe vem à boca uma palavra!

Martyrdom of the Artist

Ingrate Art! And albeit, despondent,
His eye ellipsoidal orbit burn as it may,
To exteriorize the thought he's intent,
That which in his frontal cells he stays.

Delayed is the Idea! Inspiration delays!
Here trembling, tears the paper, violent,
As the soldier who his uniform tore away
In the desperation of the last moment!

Tries to weep and dry his eyes linger!...
He's like the paralytic who, for lack
Of his own voice and in the raging hot

Fever to speak in vain, with brute fingers
To speak, his tongue pulls and pulls back,
And to his mouth even a word comes not!

Vozes de um Túmulo

Morri! E a Terra — a mãe comum — o brilho
Destes meus olhos apagou!... Assim
Tântalo, aos reais convivas, num festim,
Serviu as carnes do seu próprio filho!

Por que para este cemitério vim?!
Por quê?! Antes da vida o angusto trilho
Palmilhasse, do que este que palmilho
E que me assombra, porque não tem fim!

No ardor do sonho que o fronema exalta
Construí de orgulho ênea pirâmide alta...
Hoje, porém, que se desmoronou

A pirâmide real do meu orgulho,
Hoje que apenas sou matéria e entulho
Tenho consciência de que nada sou!

Voices from a Tomb

Dead! Earth — common mother — the glint
Of these eyes of mine extinguished!... Thus
To his regal commensals in a feast, Tantalus
Served the flesh of his own offspring!

Why come to this cemetery I must?!
Why?! I'd rather tread the narrowing
Path of life than this one be treading,
Which haunts me, for endless it's just!

In dream's ardor the phronema[*] praises,
I, proud, high aeneous[†] pyramid raised...
Today, that it did collapse so, withal,

The real pyramid of my pride, as it is,
Today that I'm only matter and debris,
I am conscious that I'm nothing at all!

---

[*] Phronema *n.* From the Greek φρόνημα, mind, spirit, thought, purpose, will (either with a positive or negative meaning).
[†] Aeneous *adj.* Bronze.

Vandalismo

Meu coração tem catedrais imensas,
Templos de priscas e longínquas datas,
Onde um nume de amor, em serenatas,
Canta a aleluia virginal das crenças.

Na ogiva fúlgida e nas colunatas
Vertem lustrais irradiações intensas
Cintilações de lâmpadas suspensas
E as ametistas e os florões e as pratas.

Como os velhos Templários medievais
Entrei um dia nessas catedrais
E nesses templos claros e risonhos...

E erguendo os gládios e brandindo as hastas,
No desespero dos iconoclastas,
Quebrei a imagem dos meus próprios sonhos!

Vandalism

My heart has cathedrals so immense,
Temples of yore and remote dates,
Where a numen of love, in serenades,
Chants a virgin halleluiah of credences.

On the fulgid ogive and colonnades
Are shed intense lustral irradiances
From suspended lamps luminescences
And amethysts, rosettes, silver plates.

As the old Templars of the medieval
Age, I once entered those cathedrals
And those clear and smiling temples…

Raising glaives, waving spears in the air,
I, like the iconoclasts in their despair,
My own dreams' image dismantled!

Versos Íntimos

Vês?! Ninguém assistiu ao formidável
Enterro de tua última quimera.
Somente a Ingratidão — esta pantera —
Foi tua companheira inseparável!

Acostuma-te à lama que te espera!
O Homem, que, nesta terra miserável,
Mora entre feras, sente inevitável
Necessidade de também ser fera.

Toma um fósforo. Acende teu cigarro!
O beijo, amigo, é a véspera do escarro,
A mão que afaga é a mesma que apedreja.

Se a alguém causa inda pena a tua chaga,
Apedreja essa vil mão que te afaga,
Escarra nessa boca que te beija!

Intimate Verses

See!? No one attended the formidable
Burial of your last chimaera to spare.
Only Ingratitude — a panther there —
Was your companion, inseparable!

Be used to a mire that is your share!
Man, who, in this land so miserable,
Lives among beasts, feels inevitable
Need to also with a beast compare.

Have a match. Light your cigarette to it!
A kiss, friend, is the eve of a sputtering,
A caressing hand is one that stones, too.

If pity for your sore in one still stands,
Stone these vile, caressing hands,
Sputter in this mouth that kisses you!

Eterna Mágoa

O homem por sobre quem caiu a praga
Da tristeza do Mundo, o homem que é triste
Para todos os séculos existe
E nunca mais o seu pesar se apaga!

Não crê em nada, pois, nada há que traga
Consolo à Mágoa, a que só ele assiste.
Quer resistir, e quanto mais resiste
Mais se lhe aumenta e se lhe afunda a chaga.

Sabe que sofre, mas o que não sabe
É que essa mágoa infinda assim, não cabe
Na sua vida, é que essa mágoa infinda

Transpõe a vida do seu corpo inerme;
E quando esse homem se transforma em verme
É essa mágoa que o acompanha ainda!

Eternal Woe

The man upon whom fell the curse for
The World's sorrow, the man who sad is,
Throughout the centuries does exist
And his grief extinguishes nevermore!

He believes in naught, for naught has bore
Solace to Woe, to which he alone assists;
Wants to resist, and the more he resists,
The more augments and deepens his sore.

He knows he suffers, but what knows not
Is that such an endless woe, it fits not
Into his life, is that this endless woe

Transposes the life of his unarmed form;
And when this man transforms into a worm
It is this woe that still follows him so!

O Lamento das Coisas

Triste, a escutar, pancada por pancada,
A sucessividade dos segundos,
Ouço, em sons subterrâneos, do Orbe oriundos,
O choro da Energia abandonada!

É a dor da Força desaproveitada,
— O cantochão dos dínamos profundos,
Que, podendo mover milhões de mundos,
Jazem ainda na estática do Nada!

É o soluço da forma ainda imprecisa...
Da transcendência que se não realiza...
Da luz que não chegou a ser lampejo...

E é, em suma, o subconsciente aí formidando
Da Natureza que parou, chorando,
No rudimentarismo do Desejo!

The Lament of Things

Tap by tap, listening with sorrowfulness
To the successivity of the seconds round,
I hear from the Orb, in subterranean sounds,
The weep of Energy in its forsakenness!

It's the aching of a Force that's fruitless,
— The plainsong of dynamos profound
Which, able to move worlds unbound,
Still lie in the statics of Nothingness!

It's the whimper of form, imprecise still…
Of transcendence which not itself fulfills…
Of light which became no sparkle of fire…

It's, in sum, the subconscious, frightful,
Of Nature which has stopped, tearful,
At the rudimentariness of Desire!

Apóstrofe à Carne

Quando eu pego nas carnes do meu rosto,
Pressinto o fim da orgânica batalha:
— Olhos que o húmus necrófago estraçalha,
Diafragmas, decompondo-se, ao sol posto...

E o Homem — negro e heteróclito composto,
Onde a alva flama psíquica trabalha,
Desagrega-se e deixa na mortalha
O tato, a vista, o ouvido, o olfato e o gosto!

Carne, feixe de mônadas bastardas,
Conquanto em flâmeo fogo efêmero ardas,
A dardejar relampejantes brilhos,

Dói-me ver, muito embora a alma te acenda,
Em tua podridão a herança horrenda,
Que eu tenho de deixar para os meus filhos!

Apostrophe[*] to the Flesh

When I grab at the flesh of my face,
I'm prescient of the organic battle end:
— Eyes the necrophagous humus rends,
Diaphragms, decomposing, at sunset late...

And Man — black and heteroclite paste,
Where the white psychic flame is agent,
Disaggregates, leaving in his cerements
Touch, sight, hearing, smell and taste!

Flesh, you of bastard monads the fascicle,
Though in ephemerous flaming fire kindle,
Fulgurant lightning gleams darting,

It ails me to see, soul-alight as you may be,
In your putridness the horrendous heredity
I have to bequeath to my offspring!

---

[*] The Portuguese noun *apóstrofe* can mean both 'the addressing of (a person or thing)' and 'invective.'

Suprême Convulsion

O equilíbrio do humano pensamento
Sofre também a súbita ruptura,
Que produz muita vez, na noite escura,
A convulsão meteórica do vento.

E a alma o obnóxio quietismo sonolento
Rasga; e, opondo-se à Inércia, é a essência pura,
É a síntese, é o transunto, é a abreviatura
De todo o ubiquitário Movimento!

Sonho, — libertação do homem cativo —
Ruptura do equilíbrio subjetivo,
Ah! foi teu beijo convulsionador

Que produziu este contraste fundo
Entre a abundância do que eu sou, no Mundo,
E o nada do meu homem interior!

Suprême Convulsion[*]

The equilibrium of human thinking
Suffers likewise the sudden rupture,
Which oft produces, in night obscure,
The wind's meteoric convulsing.

The soul an obnoxious somnolent quieting
Rends; opposing Inertia, is essence pure,
Is synthesis, is transumpt, is abbreviature[†]
Of the whole of a ubiquitous Motioning!

Dream, — liberation of man in captivity —
Rupture in the equilibrium of subjectivity,
Ah! it's your convulsing kiss which has

Produced such a profound contrast
Between the abundance that I worldly am
And the nothingness of my inner man!

---

[*] In French in the original.
[†] Abbreviature *n. obs.* Abbreviation.

A Um Gérmen

Começaste a existir, geléia crua,
E hás de crescer, no teu silêncio, tanto
Que, é natural, ainda algum dia, o pranto
Das tuas concreções plásmicas flua!

A água, em conjugação com a terra nua,
Vence o granito, deprimindo-o... O espanto
Convulsiona os espíritos, e, entanto,
Teu desenvolvimento continua!

Antes, geléia humana, não progridas
E em retrogradações indefinidas,
Volvas à antiga inexistência calma!...

Antes o Nada, oh! gérmen!, que ainda haveres
De atingir, como o gérmen de outros seres,
Ao supremo infortúnio de ser alma!

To A Germ

To exist, crude jelly, you're imbued,
And shall accrue, in silence, so might
Naturally the weeping, still sometime,
From your plasmic concretions issue!

Water, with naked earth communed,
Defeats granite, depressing it... Fright
Convulses the spirits, and in spite
Of it, your development continues!

Rather, human jelly, have no progression,
And within indefinite retrogradations,
Return to the calm inexistence of old!...

Rather Nothingness, oh! germ!, than having
To attain, as had the germ of other beings,
The supreme misfortune to be a soul!

A Floresta

Em vão com o mundo da floresta privas!...
— Todas as hermenêuticas sondagens,
Ante o hieróglifo e o enigma das folhagens,
São absolutamente negativas!

Araucárias, traçando arcos de ogivas,
Bracejamentos de álamos selvagens,
Como um convite para estranhas viagens,
Tornam todas as almas pensativas!

Há uma força vencida nesse mundo!
Todo o organismo florestal profundo
É dor viva, trancada num disfarce...

Vivem só, nele, os elementos broncos,
— As ambições que se fizeram troncos,
Porque nunca puderam realizar-se!

The Forest

In vain with the forest world be privy!...[*]
— All the hermeneutical sondages,[†]
'Fore hieroglyph and enigma of foliages,
Are most absolutely negative!

Araucarias, tracing arcs of ogives,
The branchings of alamos savage,
As an invitation to strange voyages,
Do make every one soul pensive!

There's in this world a routed vim!
Every profound forest organism
Is living pain, locked in a disguise…

Only coarse elements in it remain,
— Ambitions which trunks became,
For never could they be realized!

---

[*] Privy *adj. obs.* Familiar, intimate.
[†] Sondages *n.* Soundings.

O Poeta do Hediondo

Sofro aceleradíssimas pancadas
No coração. Ataca-me a existência
A mortificadora coalescência
Das desgraças humanas congregadas!

Em alucinatórias cavalgadas,
Eu sinto, então, sondando-me a consciência,
A ultra-inquisitorial clarividência
De todas as neuronas acordadas!

Quanto me dói no cérebro esta sonda!
Ah! Certamente, eu sou a mais hedionda
Generalização do Desconforto...

Eu sou aquele que ficou sozinho
Cantando sobre os ossos do caminho
A poesia de tudo quanto é morto!

The Poet of the Hideous

I suffer the throbs most accelerated
In the heart. Attacks my existence
The ever mortifying coalescence
Of human disgraces congregated!

In hallucinatory cavalcades,
I feel, then, probing my conscience,
The ultra-inquisitorial clairvoyance
Of all the neurones[*] awakened!

How this probe hurts me in the brain!
Ah! I am the most hideous, for certain,
Generalization of Discomfort...

I am the one who alone did stay
Singing over the bones of the way
Poetry of all that's death's worth!

---

[*] Neurones *n. var.* of neurons. (In the original, 'neurona' is a neologism by dos Anjos.)

Numa Forja

De inexplicáveis ânsias prisioneiro
Hoje entrei numa forja, ao meio-dia.
Trinta e seis graus à sombra. O éter possuía
A térmica violência de um braseiro.
Dentro, a cuspir escórias
De fúlgida limalha
Dardejando centelhas transitórias,
No horror da metalúrgica batalha
O ferro chiava e ria!

Ria, num sardonismo doloroso
De ingênita amargura,
Da qual, bruta, provinha
Como de um negro cáspio de água impura
A multissecular desesperança
De sua espécie abjeta
Condenada a uma estática mesquinha!

Ria com essa metálica tristeza
De ser na Natureza,
Onde a Matéria avança
E a Substância caminha
Aceleradamente para o gozo
Da integração completa,
Uma consciência eternamente obscura!

At a Forge

Of inexplicable anxieties a prisoner
I entered a forge, at noon today.
Thirty-six degrees in the shade. The ether laid
The thermic violence of live embers.
Inside, scoriae spitting
Of filings fulgid,
Transitory scintillations darting,
The iron, in metallurgic battle, horrid,
Creaked and laughed away!

Laughed, with a sardonicism grievous
Of ingenital bitterness,
From which, brute, descended,
As if from impure water of Caspian blackness,
Of its abject species
The multisecular desperation
To a measly static condemned!

It laughed with such metallic woe
Of being in Nature so —
Where Matter proceeds
And Substance moves, then,
Acceleratedly, to a fruition, joyous,
Of complete integration —
An eternally obscure consciousness!

O ferro continuava a chiar e a rir.
E eu nervoso, irritado,
Quase com febre, a ouvir
Cada átomo de ferro
Contra a incude esmagado
Sofrer, berrar, tinir,
Compreendia por fim que aquele berro
À substância inorgânica arrancado
Era a dor do minério castigado
Na impossibilidade de reagir!

Era um cosmos inteiro sofredor,
Cujo negror profundo
Astro nenhum exorna
Gritando na bigorna
Asperamente a sua própria dor!
Era, erguido do pó,
Inopinadamente
Para que à vida quente
Da sinergia cósmica desperte,
A ansiedade de um mundo
Doente de ser inerte,
Cansado de estar só!

The iron kept laughing and creaking.
And I, irritated, unnerved,
Almost with a fever, hearing
The atoms of iron, each,
Against the incus[*] crushed
Suffer, screech, cling,
I comprehended at last that the screech
From the inorganic substance jerked
Was the pain of the mineral punished
In its impossibility of reacting!

It was an entire cosmos suffering,
Whose profound pitch-darkness
Ornates not any one star
On the anvil crying, far
Harshly, its very own hurting!
From the dust reared
Unexpectedly, it was —
So as to wake to the warm
Life of the cosmic synergy —
A world's anxiousness
For being of inertia sickly,
Of solitude wearied!

---

[*] Incus *n. specif.* Ossicle shaped like an anvil between the malleus and stapes in the tympanum cavity of the ear. (In the original, dos Anjos uses the noun 'incude,' i.e., a form of the Latin word for anvil.)

Era a revelação
De tudo que ainda dorme
No metal bruto ou na geleia informe
Do parto primitivo da Criação!
Era o ruído-clarão,
— O ígneo jato vulcânico
Que, atravessando a absconsa cripta enorme
De minha cavernosa subconsciência,
Punha em clarividência
Intramoleculares sóis acesos
Perpetuamente às mesmas formas presos,
Agarrados à inércia do Inorgânico,
Escravos da Coesão!

Repuxavam-me a boca hórridos trismos
E eu sentia, afinal,
Essa angústia alarmante
Própria da alienação raciocinante,
Cheia de ânsias e medos
Com crispações nos dedos
Piores que os paroxismos
Da árvore que a atmosfera ultriz destronca.
A ouvir todo esse cosmos potencial,
Preso aos mineralógicos abismos
Angustiado e arquejante
A debater-se na estreiteza bronca
De um bloco de metal!

It was the revelation
Of all that's still slumberous
In the brute metal or jelly amorphous
Of the primitive birth of Creation!
It was noise-scintillation,
— The igneous jet, volcanic,
That, crossing the absconded crypt, enormous,
Of my cavernous subconscience,[*]
Showed with clairvoyance
Intramolecular lighted suns
Perpetually to the same forms clung,
Tight to the inertia of the Inorganic,
Slaves of Cohesion!

My mouth was jerked by a horrid trismus
And I felt, after all,
This anguish alarming
Proper of alienation reasoning,
Full of anxieties and fears
With twitches of the fingers
Worse than the paroxysms
Of a tree severed by atmosphere vengeful.
Hearing all this cosmos, potential,
Seized to mineralogical abysms,
Anguished and wheezing,
Struggling on the narrowness dull
Of a block of metal!

[*] Subconscience *n. misconstruction* of Subconscious.

Como que a forja tétrica
Num estridor de estrago
Executava, em lúgubre *crescendo*
A antífona assimétrica
E o incompreensível wagnerismo aziago
De seu destino horrendo!

Ao clangor de tais carmes de martírio
Em cismas negras eu recaio imerso
Buscando no delírio
De uma imaginação convulsionada
Mais revolta talvez do que a onda atlântica,
Compreender a semântica
Dessa aleluia bárbara gritada
Às margens glacialíssimas do Nada
Pelas coisas mais brutas do Universo!

As if the forge, gruesome,
In a stridor damageable
Executed, in a lugubrious *crescendo*,
The asymmetric antiphon
And ominous Wagnerism incomprehensible
Of its destiny, horrendous!

At the clangor of such carmina of martirization
Into black misgivings I relapse immersed
Pursuing, with the deliration
Of an imagination so convulsing,
Stormier perhaps than the billow of the Atlantic,
To comprehend the semantics
Of this barbaric halleluiah yelled being,
On Nothingness's most glacial margins,
By the most brute things of the Universe!

Vítima do Dualismo

Ser miserável dentre os miseráveis
— Carrego em minhas células sombrias
Antagonismos irreconciliáveis
E as mais opostas idiossincrasias!

Muito mais cedo do que imagináveis
Eis-vos, minha alma, enfim, dada às bravias
Cóleras dos dualismos implacáveis
E à gula negra das antinomias!

Psique biforme, o Céu e o Inferno absorvo...
Criação a um tempo escura e cor-de-rosa,
Feita dos mais variáveis elementos,

Ceva-se em minha carne, como um corvo,
A simultaneidade ultramonstruosa
De todos os contrastes famulentos!

Victim of Dualism

A miserable being amid the miserable
— I carry within my cells, so eerie,
Antagonisms as such irreconcilable
And the most opposed idiosyncrasies!

Much sooner than would be imaginable,
Behold my soul, why, prone to savagery
Of cholers from dualisms implacable
And the black gluttony of antinomies!

Biform psyche, I absorb Hell and Heaven...
Creation at once of rose and obscurity,
From the most variable elements cast,

It feasts in my flesh, just like a raven,
The ultramonstruous simultaneity
Of every one of the famished contrasts!

Ao Luar

Quando, à noite, o Infinito se levanta
À luz do luar, pelos caminhos quedos
Minha tátil intensidade é tanta
Que eu sinto a alma do Cosmos nos meus dedos!

Quebro a custódia dos sentidos tredos
E a minha mão, dona, por fim, de quanta
Grandeza o Orbe estrangula em seus segredos,
Todas as coisas íntimas suplanta!

Penetro, agarro, ausculto, apreendo, invado,
Nos paroxismos da hiperestesia,
O Infinitésimo e o Indeterminado...

Transponho ousadamente o átomo rude
E, transmudado em rutilância fria,
Encho o Espaço com a minha plenitude!

In the Moonlight

When it is risen, at night, Infinity
In the moonlight, by paths of a quietus
Such is my own tactile intensity
My fingers feel the soul of the Cosmos!

I break the custody of senses insidious
And my hand, at last, with the mastery
Of all grandeur strangled by secret modus
Of the Orb, supplants every intimacy!

I pierce, grasp, listen, apprehend, invade,
With my hyperesthesia in paroxysms,
The Infinitesimal and the Indeterminate...

I transcend audaciously the atom rude
And, by a cold rutilant metamorphism,
Replenish the Space with my plenitude!

Anseio

Que sou eu, neste ergástulo das vidas
Danadamente, a soluçar de dor?!
— Trinta trilhões de células vencidas,
Nutrindo uma efeméride inferior.

Branda, entanto, a afagar tantas feridas,
A áurea mão taumatúrgica do Amor
Traça, nas minhas formas carcomidas,
A estrutura de um mundo superior!

Alta noite, esse mundo incoerente,
Essa elementaríssima semente
Do que hei de ser, tenta transpor o Ideal...

Grita em meu grito, alarga-se em meu hausto,
E, ai! como eu sinto no esqueleto exausto
Não poder dar-lhe vida material!

Anxiety

In this ergastulum of lives doomed,
What am I, sobbing with woe?!
— Thirty trillion cells subdued,
An inferior ephemeris nursing so.

Bland, yet, caressing many a wound,
Love's thaumaturgic hand of gold
Traces, in my forms ever ruined,
The structure of a superior world!

Late night, this world incoherent,
Of this most elementary semen[*]
I shall be, tries the Ideal to exceed...

It cries in my cry, in my draught prolongs,
Alas! how in my exhausted skeleton
Ails me, not to material life concede it!

---

[*] Seed.

O Último Número

Hora da minha morte. Hirta, ao meu lado,
A Ideia estertorava-se... No fundo
Do meu entendimento moribundo
Jazia o Último Número cansado.

Era de vê-lo, imóvel, resignado,
Tragicamente de si mesmo oriundo,
Fora da sucessão, estranho ao mundo,
Como o reflexo fúnebre do Incriado.

Bradei: — Que fazes ainda no meu crânio?
E o Último Número, atro e subterrâneo,
Parecia dizer-me: "É tarde, amigo!

Pois que a minha autogênita Grandeza
Nunca vibrou em tua língua presa,
Não te abandono mais! Morro contigo!"

The Last Number

Hour of my death. Stiff, by my side,
The Idea throed, stertorous... In the end
Bottom of my moribund understanding
Was laid the Last Number, all tired.

One ought to see it, immobile, resigned,
Tragically from its very self originating,
Out of succession, the world estranging,
As funereal reflex of the Undesigned.[*]

I cried: — What yet you do in my cranium?
And the Last Number, dark, subterraneous,
Seemed to tell me so: "Friend, it's late!

Inasmuch as my autogenic Magnitude
Never vibrated in your tongue abstruse,
I abandon you no more! With you I fade!"

---

[*] Uncreated.

Critical assessments on Augusto dos Anjos

Hermes Fontes

Augusto dos Anjos is, in his book *Eu*, the affirmation of a great spirit and the announcement of a great poet. [The book] depends on many readings. The first stuns, the second enthuses, the third sensibilizes, the fourth enchants and conducts, not rarely, to tears and ecstasy. And even the extravagant and preposterous things acquire new forces, flashes of lightning which have passed by our dazzled and obnubilated sight. . . . We would not exchange, for example, the whole work of many conventionally great poets of ours, for the depth and serenity of these two impressive lines: *"The very solidarity rather subjective/ Of the entirety of species suffering."* Or these: *"In the crepuscular soul of my race/ As if a very vocation for Disgrace,/ An ancestral tropism for Misfortune."*

("Literary Chronicle, in *Diário de Notícias*,
Rio de Janeiro, July 16th, 1912. 49-52)

Antônio Torres

I come to speak neither of Baudelaire nor of "Une Charogne." The Poet of Death to which I refer is rather another one.

He's a barbarian, born in the shade of the buriti groves of Paraíba and recently deceased on the misty mountains of Minas [Gerais]. I speak of Augusto dos Anjos.

He was a strange, *sui generis* poet in Brazil. . . . Master of a scientific culture superior to that of his age and to the milieu in which he studied; knowing how to versify with elegance and brightness; possessing a true soul of poet and idealist; he was a convinced monist, at least in his early life. One could see that the abundant literature of Haeckel and Spencer had left a deep groove in his intelligence.

In the world he ever saw the cosmic combinations, the elementary alliances, the seismic convulsions, the telluric and sidereal revolutions, the amalgam of all the latent forces of the Universe, submitted to the fatality of physical and biological laws, and tending to the harmony and unity of Life.

("The Poet of Death,"
in *Jornal do Comércio*, Rio de Janeiro, Dec. 27th, 1914. 52-59)

Critical assessments on Augusto dos Anjos

Álvaro Lins

Augusto dos Anjos only participated in the ephemeral of his time to the extent of the indispensable, to that minimum in which all men are obligate to participate in their ambient. Do not seek in his work normal currents of influences, nor aesthetic affiliations. . . . In Augusto dos Anjos, naturalism is the creed, materialism is the doctrine, with a sentiment which doesn't exceed the visible and the sensitive save poetically, and his regard is not particularly turned to metaphysical mysteries, but to the subsoil of human existence. Antichristian *par excellence*, the circle within which he moved was the physical nothing, and thence he extracted, from the tragic of that void, the substance of his thought and the matter of his verses. . . . Nevertheless, his genuine position is that of a solitary, for whom there was neither tomorrow nor hope. He was alone in the world – with his enormous, dreadful and terrible *Eu* – to cultivate melancholy, grief, disenchantment, to sing death and the poetry of dead things. . . .

Our old poets . . . cannot be appreciated without historical considerations, without a connection with their time and respective literary currents. Augusto dos Anjos, however, is illuminated by a projection of permanent presentness, which incessantly casts him towards the future, as being more and more alive, with his chant, as it were, appropriate to directly touch the intelligence, the heart and the senses of men from all times.

Of all time, and even of all ages. Now this is not praise, but evidence of a weak part, detestable under certain aspects, in the work of Augusto dos Anjos. He has, in fact, two faces: that of the authentic poet and that of the vulgarly sensational poet; that of the artist, with an enormous richness of thought and sensibility, and that of the artificer, with the garish garb of a precarious scientific terminology. We find in him the purest literary value and the most horrendous bad taste. Sometimes, the bad taste in Augusto dos Anjos is so absolute, so frightful, so irritating, that a reader of exquisite taste can make the mistake of despising him because he no longer has patience to pursue the true poet within that confusion between beauty and vulgarity. There are, then, two Augusto dos Anjos, and unfortunately the most loved and appreciated by the wide public is the least estimable one. The wide public, like the adolescents, preferably esteem in Augusto dos Anjos the sensationalistic poems, which are the most banal, the verses which present the false brilliance of the pompous, extravagant, eccentric and spectacular words....

Nevertheless, if the nomenclature of the physical and natural sciences adds nothing to the value of Augusto dos Anjos' poetry, and rather spoils it by the prosaism and bad taste to which it is many times submitted, the scientific spirit, the ability of contemplating reality with a scientific spirit, which is first of all an intellectual attitude, gives to the poet's vision an extraordinary amplitude, as an instrument of penetration and acuity. If it kills puerile illusions, it constructs solid and profound thoughts. The scientific spirit opened up to the poet perspectives and angles until then unknown in our letters. There, indeed, science harmonizes with poetry: as an indirect auxiliary, as an impulse for the poetic plunge into the mystery of natural phenomena. With the philosophical and scientific spirit, and with his personal singularity, Augusto dos Anjos turned into the Brazilian poet whose thought attained the highest height, density and consistency....

By way of intelligence, the vision of Augusto dos Anjos was materialistic, constructed upon doctrines from philosophy and science, which he incompletely studied, but of which he impregnated himself owing to the naturality with which they adjusted to the complexion of his human nature. By way of sensibility and imagination, nevertheless, he was ever unsatisfied and unquiet, sensing in the very cosmos – a word by him so esteemed and used – the presence of mysteries, undecipherable with the codes of philosophy and science, the presence everywhere of those reasons the reason cannot know. The two tendencies are visible in all pages of *Eu*, if one compares some poems with others, and sometimes sections of the same poem. In certain parts, he is affirmative, dogmatic, conceptual, sure of himself and of his thoughts; in others, he interrogates, doubts, despairs before the unknown, struggles with anxieties, in a state of perplexity in face of the mystery, which a poet is presentient of even in the simplest, most immediate and visible things.

("Augusto dos Anjos: Poeta Moderno," in *Jornal de Crítica*, 4ª Série (Rio de Janeiro, José Olímpio, 1951), 118-123)

Otto Maria Carpeaux

There were some few dedicated readers who succeeded in vindicating and reestablishing the true greatness of Augusto dos Anjos: Álvaro Lins, Antônio Houaiss, Francisco de Assis Barbosa (and, as in the altarpieces of medieval churches the painter dared to place on the last corner his self-portrait, so I dare to place at the end of this list my own name). Reading and rereading *Eu*, we always discover new, strange and admirable things. The bad taste of scientific and pseudo-scientific expressions? Augusto dos Anjos has the extraordinary power of revealing an occult sense in the sounds of those barbarous words, which add a new *frisson* to his gruesome and profoundly moving visions. His surprising and extravagant rhymes open up never-before-seen horizons; he is like the English *metaphysical poets* whom he did not know. He can also give metaphysical flavor to proper names; and even one who ignores that the Agra's home, in Recife, by the end of Buarque de Macedo Bridge, is the morgue, feels all the tremor of menacing death in the verse: "Recife. Buarque de Macedo Bridge...," a tremor due to the terrifying and as-if-definitive period after the word "Recife," a caesura that is the dividing line between life and the end of life.

There are in Augusto dos Anjos countless cases like this, of a discovery of a new sense in words. Not always do we clearly realize the reasons for our admiration. . . . When Augusto dos Anjos died, the sky of Brazilian poetry was obscured as if by darkness at midday. Nobody acknowledged him. Today, Brazilian literature seems, once more, obscured by darkness. But who knows if it is not found, unrecognized, among us – or even far from us – the great poet who can tell how this people suffers and foresee a new dawn?

("Presentation," in Dos Anjos, Augusto.
Toda a Poesia. Com um estudo crítico de Ferreira Gullar.
Rio de Janeiro: Paz e Terra, 1976, on flaps)

Alexei Bueno

The poetry of Augusto dos Anjos impresses us, even today, by the extreme specificity of the individual who composed it, by the character of extreme independence, almost of spontaneous generation, with which it irrupted in the panorama of Brazilian literature. In fact, that independence of the thinking individual, such as or more astonishing than that of the poet he was, immediately justifies the title of the *I*, all the more proving the acute self-consciousness of its author. . . .

What seems to us undeniable in the case of Augusto dos Anjos is the primordial sincerity of his intellectual and even emotional adhesion to the postulates of that worldview, residing there, including his astonishing ability to write high poetry from the like, a fact that eliminates any suspicion of a poseur's or a pedant's temperament in his exhibition of scientific thought. If in the question of the lexicon, above all in his prose, perhaps, it seems to us that the poet succumbed to an irresistible compulsion to épater *le bourgeois* with his overwhelming culture, it equally seems to us that in his poetry the use of the same vocabulary, otherwise mitigated in the last phase, is the fruit of an absolutely authentic flow of sensibility, not only of the concepts inherent in the vocables, but also of the strange and musical incantatory power of their phonetic framework. The presence of a similar use even in his personal correspondence, written with no intention of making literature, rather proves to us how natural such a process was for him, notwithstanding the strangest tone it acquires in the heart of a familiar epistolography.

Part of the incomprehension which was created around that use of scientific vocabulary, most particularly names of species and philosophical terms, comes, in truth, from a certain mental laziness of the reader in relation to vocables which cause strangeness and whose utilization seems preposterous and useless. The incorporation, nevertheless, of those minute beings, of those microorganisms which are as strange to us as the very names that designate them, lies perfectly within the plan of the poet, prolocutor of the essence of all beings, and not of man alone. The originality of that position is marked by the sonorous originality of the names of species.

("Augusto dos Anjos: Origins of a Poetics,"
in Dos Anjos, Augusto, *Obra Completa*.
Rio de Janeiro, Editora Nova Aguilar, 1994, 21-23)

www.ingramcontent.com/pod-product-compliance
Lightning Source LLC
Chambersburg PA
CBHW051840090426
42736CB00011B/1891